The Actor's Book of Quotes

Words of Wisdom for Performing Artists

The Actor's Book of Quotes

**Words of Wisdom
for Performing Artists**

Mike Kimmel

Copyright © 2023 Mike Kimmel

All rights reserved.
No portion of this book may be reproduced or transmitted in any form or by any means, electronic or mechanical, including photocopying, recording, or by any information storage or retrieval system, except for the inclusion of brief quotations in reviews.

ISBN 978-1-953057-13-6 (paperback)
ISBN 978-1-953057-14-3 (hardcover)
ISBN 978-1-953057-15-0 (ebook)

Library of Congress Control Number 2022922323

The Actor's Book of Quotes:
Words of Wisdom for Performing Artists
The Professional Actor Series: Book 4

Ben Rose Creative Arts
New York - Los Angeles

Publisher's Cataloging-in-Publication Data
provided by Five Rainbows Cataloging Services

Names: Kimmel, Mike, author.
Title: The actor's book of quotes : words of wisdom for performing artists / Mike Kimmel.
Description: Los Angeles : Ben Rose Creative Arts, 2023. | Series: Professional actor series, bk. 4.
Identifiers: LCCN 2022922323 (print) | ISBN 978-1-953057-13-6 (paperback) | ISBN 978-1-953057-14-3 (hardcover) | ISBN 978-1-953057-15-0 (ebook)
Subjects: LCSH: Quotations. | Monologues. | Acting--Auditions. | Performing arts. | Arts--Study and teaching. | BISAC: REFERENCE / Quotations. | PERFORMING ARTS / Monologues & Scenes. | PERFORMING ARTS / Acting & Auditioning.
Classification: LCC PN2080 .K56 2023 (print) | LCC PN2080 (ebook) | DDC 812/.6--dc23.

Interior design by Booknook.biz

For Joyce Storey

Table of Contents

Introduction	xi
Actors' Quotations	1
Advertising and Commercials	14
Aging and Remaining Significant	17
Audiences	21
Auditions	26
Authenticity and Being Yourself	30
Awards	32
Awareness	35
Beauty	37
Believing	41
Circumstances	43
Comedy	45
Complacency and Comfort Zones	50
Contribution	52
Creativity	54
Criticism	56
Decisions	59
Depression	61

Discipline, Consistency, and Preparation	63
Doubts	65
Drama	67
Dreams	69
Early Work	71
Ego, Pride, and Humility	76
Enthusiasm	78
Envy, Comparison, and Competition	80
Exceptionalism	82
Excesses	84
Failure … and Bouncing Back!	86
Faith	89
Fame	91
Family	98
Fear	101
Feelings and Emotions	104
Focus	106
Getting Started	108
Goals	110
Happiness	112
Hard Work	116
Health and Fitness	119

A Higher Power	121
Hooray for Hollywood!	123
Humor	126
Iconic Roles	129
Imagination	133
Individuality	135
Life	140
Love	142
Luck	144
Marriage	146
Men and Women	149
Mistakes	155
Money	157
Movies	161
The Mutual Admiration Society	166
Negativity	172
No Biz Like Show Biz!	174
Optimism and Pessimism	179
Opportunities	181
Overcoming Your Past	183
Patience. Persistence. Perseverance.	184
Possible vs. Impossible	187

Preparation and Rehearsal	190
Purpose and Fulfillment	192
Rejection	194
Risk	197
Scripts	198
Self-Awareness and Self-Reflection	201
Self-Confidence	203
Self-Development and Self-Realization	205
Self-Esteem	207
Self-Reliance	210
Service	212
Simplicity	214
Solitude	216
Staying on Track	218
Study	219
Success	221
Survival Jobs	223
Taking Small Steps Daily	226
Teamwork	228
Technique	231
Television	239
Theater	243

Thinking Bigger	248
Treating People Right	250
Typecasting	254
Visualization	257
A Request	259
Performing Arts Books in this Series	260
About Mike Kimmel	261

"The wisdom of the wise, and the experience of ages,
may be preserved by quotations."
~ Benjamin Disraeli ~

Introduction

There have been many wonderful collections of quotations compiled through the years. What makes this one unique is that it's created specifically for one profession: Acting.

When I was a kid growing up in the Beautiful Bronx, New York, we had a saying: "You're special and unique … just like everyone else." As a longtime actor and acting coach, that quote has always resonated with me. It reminds me that we're never truly alone in our journey through this world—and the next. Our problems are not unique. Billions of others before us have experienced—and overcome—the same challenges we face today.

Those unseen "others" who preceded us have always been a source of strength, inspiration, and comfort to me. I've been collecting their quotes for many years. Through their writings, speeches, and interviews, they've provided practical advice, life strategies, wisdom, and humor to overcome challenges, stay motivated, and keep moving forward on my actor's journey. They've given me plenty to think about. They've given me plenty to laugh about too. They've given me plenty.

I hope you will enjoy, apply, and benefit from the quotes contained in this book. They were bequeathed to us. They have been entrusted to our care by some of the wisest and most accomplished women and men we've never met. The quotations are from actors and non-actors alike—including professionals in science, business, government, education, literature, philosophy, and the visual arts. The topics, however, are of particular interest to performing artists.

If you have the time and the inclination, try memorizing a few of the quotations in this book. You can then pass them along to others who will benefit from these pearls of wisdom, as well. I wish you all the very best on your actor's journey—and every other journey you will take.

And always remember, you are never alone.

Mike Kimmel
Los Angeles, California

Actors' Quotations

"Don't just aspire to make a living. Aspire to make a difference."
~ Denzel Washington ~

"I don't know what is better than the work that is given to the actor—to teach the human heart the knowledge of itself."
~ Laurence Olivier ~

"I'm not funny. What I am is brave."
~ Lucille Ball ~

"The trouble with the rat race is that even if you win, you're still a rat."
~ Lily Tomlin ~

"I'm too tall to be a girl. I'm between a chick and a broad."
~ Julia Roberts ~

"I grew up with a lot of boys. I probably have a lot of testosterone for a woman."
~ Cameron Diaz ~

"I keep working because I learn something new all the time."
~ Clint Eastwood ~

"The work is the most fun. It seems illicit how much fun it is."
~ Meryl Streep ~

"You've achieved success in your field when you don't know whether what you're doing is work or play."
~ Warren Beatty ~

"I am where I am because I believe in all possibilities."
~ Whoopi Goldberg ~

"Be so good that they can't ignore you."
~ Steve Martin ~

"Sometimes the better an actor is, the less he's noticed."
~ Kate Jackson ~

"I've always had this idea that I wanted movies to make people better not worse."
~ Jodie Foster ~

"There's not much to say about acting but this. Never settle back on your heels. Never relax. If you relax, the audience relaxes. And always mean everything you say."
~ James Cagney ~

"The best actors do not let the wheels show."
~ Henry Fonda ~

"Actually, the ultimate in any art is never to show the wheels grinding. The essence of bad acting, for example, is shouting. (Spencer) Tracy never shouts. He's the greatest movie actor there ever was."
~ Richard Widmark ~

"I'm an actor—it's not brain surgery. If I do my job right, people won't ask for their money back."
~ Sean Connery ~

"My acting range has always been something between the two extremes of 'raises left eyebrow' and 'raises right eyebrow.'"
~ Roger Moore ~

"My husband was actually very keen that I would become a Bond girl."
~ Judi Dench ~

"Great actors try to dismiss all ideas from their conscious mind in order to provide an experience that is real."
~ Mark Rylance ~

"My folks came to the U.S. as immigrants, aliens, and became citizens. I was born in Boston, a citizen, went to Hollywood and became an alien."
~ Leonard Nimoy ~

"I think life is a series of difficult choices, and then life throws the inevitable curveball. I think more and more, getting through life is finding a sense of humor and being this wise person who laughs at everything."
~ Glenn Close ~

"If at the end of the day, people look at it and say, oh, yeah, I liked his stuff, or for the most part I liked his stuff, or I've enjoyed watching some of the things he's done, that's all I can hope for."
~ Joe Mantegna ~

"People say I'm a one-note actor, but the way I figure it, those other guys are just looking for that one right note."
~ Joel McCrea ~

"I don't care whether or not people like me or dislike me. I'm not on Earth to win a popularity contest. I'm here to be the best human being I possibly can be."
~ Tab Hunter ~

"The most dangerous thing for an actor is to refuse to listen to anyone else, to feel you know more than anybody."
~ Rock Hudson ~

"The advice I would give to someone is to not take anyone's advice."
~ Eddie Murphy ~

"Once you get rid of the idea that you must please other people before you please yourself, and you begin to follow your own instincts, only then can you be successful. You become more satisfied, and when you are, other people will tend to be satisfied by what you do."
~ Raquel Welch ~

"If someone says 'Give me one word of advice,' I say 'be fearless.' And knowing without any shadow of a doubt that what they have to give—who they are—is totally unique and not shared by anybody else. And to believe in that uniqueness. It took me decades before I developed courage as an actor."
~ Patrick Stewart ~

"As an actor, there's no autonomy, unless you're prepared to risk the possibility of starving."
~ Ben Kingsley ~

"As actors, we're all encouraged to feel that each job is the last job. They plant some little electrode in your head at an early stage and you think, 'Be grateful, be grateful, be grateful.'"
~ Daniel Day-Lewis ~

"So I had to be careful. I recognized the responsibility that, whether I liked it or not, I had to accept whatever the obligation was. That was to behave in a manner, to carry myself in such a professional way, as if there ever is a reflection, it's a positive one."
~ Sidney Poitier ~

"My mother taught me that your presentation is an expression of how much you care about yourself and those around you."
~ Lupita Nyong'o ~

"To fulfill a dream, to be allowed to sweat over lonely labor, to be given the chance to create, is the meat and potatoes of life."
~ Bette Davis ~

"I'm not an actor because I want my picture taken. I'm an actor because I want to be part of the human exchange."
~ Frances McDormand ~

"For beautiful eyes, look for the good in others; for beautiful lips, speak only words of kindness; and for poise, walk with the knowledge that you are never alone."
~ Audrey Hepburn ~

"Being a sex symbol is a heavy load to carry, especially when one is very tired, hurt and bewildered."
~ Clara Bow ~

"All I wanted was just what everybody else wants, you know, to be loved."
~ Rita Hayworth ~

"The two big advantages I had at birth were being born wise and to have been born in poverty."
~ Sophia Loren ~

"Sophia Loren plays peasants. I play ladies."
~ Gina Lollobrigida ~

"I'm drawn to emotionally damaged characters because there is more to unlock."
~ Helena Bonham Carter ~

"Before we ever had a script or anything, I was attracted to the idea of playing a character that housed within himself two opposing traits."
~ Peter Falk ~

"I don't think of myself as a TV actor. I think of myself as a film, television and Off-Off-Off-Off Broadway actor."
~ David Duchovny ~

"To be someone you must last."
~ Ruth Gordon ~

"There is a strange pecking order among actors.
Theatre actors look down on film actors, who look down on
TV actors. Thank God for reality shows, or we wouldn't have
anybody to look down on."
~ George Clooney ~

"When I was fourteen years old, I decided I could cook.
It was either that or puberty."
~ Dom DeLuise ~

"I wasn't born an actress, you know. Events made me one."
~ Jean Harlow ~

"I don't want people to know what I'm actually like.
It's not good for an actor."
~ Jack Nicholson ~

"I don't want people to know me.
I want them to believe my version."
~ William Shatner ~

"I remember having my own apartment and a little used
white Mustang car and three thousand dollars in the bank,
driving down Sunset Boulevard thinking,
'Wow, it doesn't get any better than this!'"
~ Cheryl Ladd ~

"People say women shouldn't have long hair over a certain age,
but I've never done what everyone says."
~ Jane Seymour ~

"I dropped out of college my junior year to do *Saturday Night Live*, and I didn't even consult my parents. They were very supportive because they had no choice."
~ *Julia Louis-Dreyfus* ~

"If a face like Ingrid Bergman's looks at you as though you're adorable, everybody does. You don't have to act very much."
~ *Humphrey Bogart* ~

"I hate Sunday, I can't wait for Monday so I can go back to work again."
~ *Ingrid Bergman* ~

"I stopped believing in Santa Claus when I was six. Mother took me to see him in a department store and he asked for my autograph."
~ *Shirley Temple* ~

"I was born at the age of twelve on a Metro-Goldwyn-Mayer lot."
~ *Judy Garland* ~

"The hardest job kids face today is learning good manners without seeing any."
~ *Fred Astaire* ~

"You only live once, but if you do it right, once is enough."
~ *Mae West* ~

"Life engenders life. Energy creates energy. It is by spending oneself that one becomes rich."
~ *Sarah Bernhardt* ~

"Sometimes good things fall apart
so better things can fall together."
~ Marilyn Monroe ~

"I was always a character actor. I just looked like
Little Red Riding Hood."
~ Paul Newman ~

"I was always very dramatic—my family would probably use the word 'dramatic'—as a child. Always putting on performances, making everyone come watch, and pay to watch. I was very business-savvy as a child."
~ Margot Robbie ~

"To get folks to like you, as a screen player, I mean, I figured you had to sort of be their ideal. I don't mean a handsome knight riding a white horse, but a fella who answered the description of a right guy."
~ Gary Cooper ~

"To be good, you need to believe in what you're doing."
~ Billy Crystal ~

"I found out that important and serious are not the same thing"
~ Sam Waterston ~

"I've played a lot of untalented people."
~ Vanessa Kirby ~

"Acting is happy agony."
~ Alec Guinness ~

"One of the ways I think I gain fodder for characters is by watching people."
~ *Edie Falco* ~

"I prefer full-length camera shots because the body can act better than the face."
~ *Alec Guinness* ~

"There's such an emphasis on having a character be likable. I don't think it would be helpful if I worried about that. I mean, not everyone's likable."
~ *Adam Driver* ~

"Here's a rule I recommend: Never practice two vices at once."
~ *Tallulah Bankhead* ~

"I wasn't really naked. I simply didn't have any clothes on."
~ *Josephine Baker* ~

"The only reason they come to see me is that I know that life is great—and they know I know it."
~ *Clark Gable* ~

"Jerry Seinfeld made a puddle, I stepped in it, and wonderful things happened."
~ *Jason Alexander* ~

"Outside of a dog, a book is man's best friend. Inside of a dog, it's too dark to read."
~ *Groucho Marx* ~

"I don't remember ever having a bad meal."
~ Harpo Marx ~

"Hollywood is a film industry, a film business. I don't approach my career in that way. I see it as 'art,' and I become involved in films that ring my bell."
~ Sissy Spacek ~

"By instinct I'm an adventurer; by choice I'd like to be a writer; by pure, unadulterated luck, I'm an actor."
~ Errol Flynn ~

"I have the terrible feeling that, because I am wearing a white beard and am sitting in the back of the theatre, you expect me to tell you the truth about something. These are the cheap seats, not Mount Sinai."
~ Orson Welles ~

"It's always good to take something that's happened in your life and make something of it comedically."
~ Larry David ~

"I can't say I ever wanted to become an entertainer. I already was one, sort of, around the house, at school, doing my magic tricks, throwing my voice and doing Popeye impersonations. People thought I was funny … so I kind of took entertaining for granted. It was inevitable that I'd start giving little performances."
~ Johnny Carson ~

"You can't stay mad at somebody who makes you laugh."
~ Jay Leno ~

"I was street-smart, but unfortunately
the street was Rodeo Drive."
~ Carrie Fisher ~

"You treat anyone normally, and they'll treat you normally back."
~ Henry Cavill ~

"I won't be wronged. I won't be insulted. I won't be laid
a-hand on. I don't do these things to other people, and
I require the same from them."
~ John Wayne ~

"When I'm pushed, I shove."
~ James Garner ~

"There's only one thing worse than a man who doesn't have
strong likes and dislikes, and that's a man who has strong likes
and dislikes without the courage to voice them."
~ Tony Randall ~

"I'm not of the can-kicking, shovel-carrying, ear-scratching,
torn T-shirt school of acting. There are very few real men in the
movies these days. Yet being a real man is the most important
quality an actor can offer on the screen."
~ Yul Brynner ~

"I'm one of those people you hate because of genetics.
It's the truth."
~ Brad Pitt ~

"Don't think for a moment that I'm really like any of the characters I play. That's why it's called acting."
~ Leonardo DiCaprio ~

"I've always had the same principle for choosing roles, which is to try and make movies that I would pay to see. As I get older, that's meant different things."
~ Scarlett Johansson ~

"I don't think I've been bored, ever. I've always been working on two or three things at a time; whether it was in the early days, or whatever, I was always working on something."
~ Danny DeVito ~

"One thing I am convinced of is that the more you do, the more you can do."
~ Lauren Bacall ~

"People always want me to talk about Wonder Woman, so I do."
~ Lynda Carter ~

"I was a huge comic book fan, and I still am."
~ Jason Momoa ~

"I call myself an actor. I mean, when did you last see a doctress?"
~ Viola Davis ~

"I gravitate towards gravitas."
~ Morgan Freeman ~

Advertising and Commercials

"Commerciality is ruining the Super Bowl ads this year."
~ *Steve Martin* ~

"In my world—advertising—the Super Bowl is judgment day. If politicians have Election Day and Hollywood has the Oscars, advertising has the Super Bowl."
~ *Jerry Della Femina* ~

"Unfortunately, most Super Bowl commercials end up being unmemorable. Costly mistakes for brands and creative flameouts for advertising firms."
~ *Peter Diamandis* ~

"Much of the messy advertising you see on television today is the product of committees. Committees can criticize advertisements, but they should never be allowed to create them."
~ *David Ogilvy* ~

"The number of agency people required to shoot a commercial on location is in direct proportion to the mean temperature of the location."
~ *Shelby Page* ~

"A lot of advertising has gotten worse. I think it's kind of lost its nerve, to be honest with you. I feel like the advertising of the '60s, they were nervier. You know why? Because there was less at stake."
~ *Jerry Seinfeld* ~

"People worship anyone in the entertainment industry. You can be a used-car salesman and have a television commercial on the local station, and that makes you a celebrity."
~ Mark Foster ~

"The only reason I made a commercial for American Express was to pay for my American Express bill."
~ Peter Ustinov ~

"The philosophy behind much advertising is based on the old observation that every man is really two men—the man he is and the man he wants to be."
~ William Feather ~

"The secret of all effective advertising is not the creation of new and tricky words and pictures, but one of putting familiar words and pictures into new relationships."
~ Leo Burnett ~

"Advertising is to a genuine article what manure is to land—it largely increases the product."
~ P.T. Barnum ~

"The irony is, the advertising industry knows everyone hates what they produce. This is why they keep looking for new ways to force people to stay tuned."
~ Simon Sinek ~

"Few people at the beginning of the nineteenth century needed an adman to tell them what they wanted."
~ John Kenneth Galbraith ~

"The advertising world had space men in it
before spacemen existed."
~ *Fred Allen* ~

"In advertising, not to be different is virtually suicidal."
~ *Bill Bernback* ~

"The advertisement is one of the most interesting
and difficult of modern literary forms."
~ *Aldous Huxley* ~

"Advertising is the greatest art form of the 20th century."
~ *Marshall McLuhan* ~

"Promise, loud promise, is the soul of an advertisement."
~ *Samuel Johnson* ~

"Let advertisers spend the same amount of money improving
their product that they do on advertising and
they wouldn't have to advertise it."
~ *Will Rogers* ~

"Stop advertising and start innovating."
~ *Seth Godin* ~

"Give them quality. That's the best kind of advertising."
~ *Milton Hershey* ~

"I saw a subliminal advertising executive, but only for a second."
~ *Steven Wright* ~

Aging and Remaining Significant

"It is strange that the years teach us patience; that the shorter our time, the greater our capacity for waiting."
~ Elizabeth Taylor ~

"When people tell you how young you look, they are also telling you how old you are."
~ Cary Grant ~

"You know you're getting old when all the names in your black book have M.D. after them."
~ Harrison Ford ~

"You are more thoughtful because you don't act as quickly anymore. When I turned seventy, it was the first time I felt young for my age. Fifty dropped on me like a ton of bricks—there is something about that number—but when seventy came along, I felt good about it."
~ Jack Nicholson ~

"I think we are able to keep active provided we approach our lives with creativity. I think the mere fact that we keep doing is self-creating."
~ Jessica Tandy ~

"It is sad to grow old but nice to ripen."
~ Brigitte Bardot ~

"A woman at twenty is like ice, at thirty she is warm,
and at forty she is hot."
~ *Gina Lollobrigida* ~

"The older you get, the more fragile you understand life to be.
I think that's good motivation for getting out of bed
joyfully each day."
~ *Julia Roberts* ~

"Life is short, even for those who live a long time,
and we must live for the few who know and appreciate us,
who judge and absolve us, and for whom we have the same
affection and indulgence."
~ *Sarah Bernhardt* ~

"I'm a tough old broad from Brooklyn. I intend to go
on acting until I'm ninety and they won't need to
paste my face with make-up."
~ *Barbara Stanwyck* ~

"The tragedy of life is not that it ends so soon, but that
we wait so long to begin it."
~ *W.M. Lewis* ~

"Life is available to anyone no matter what age.
All you have to do is grab it."
~ *Art Carney* ~

"As I've gotten older, I've found that I can have men as friends.
I used to not be able to."
~ *Farrah Fawcett* ~

"If you survive long enough, you're revered—
rather like an old building."
~ *Katharine Hepburn* ~

"One starts to get young at the age of sixty, and then it is too late.
~ *Pablo Picasso* ~

"I suddenly find out that I'm sixty, and I get shocked
by the number, because I feel like I'm twenty."
~ *Ursula Andress* ~

"More than anything else, I'd like to be an old man with
a good face, like Hitchcock or Picasso."
~ *Sean Connery* ~

"You can either grow old gracefully or begrudgingly.
I chose both."
~ *Roger Moore* ~

"You know when you're young and you see a play in high
school, and the guys all have gray in their hair and they're
trying to be old men and they have no idea what that's like?
It's just that stupid the other way around."
~ *Clint Eastwood* ~

"You can only hold your stomach in for so many years."
~ *Burt Reynolds* ~

"Something funny happens as you get older,
you don't hold back so much."
~ *James Garner* ~

"Hollywood is a place where the stars twinkle until they wrinkle."
~ Victor Mature ~

"How old would you be if you didn't know how old you are?"
~ Satchel Paige ~

"When you're happy, you don't count the years."
~ Ginger Rogers ~

"I'm seventeen and I'm crazy. My uncle says the two always go together. When people ask your age, he said, always say seventeen and insane."
~ Ray Bradbury ~

"Aging is an inevitable process. I surely wouldn't want to grow younger. The older you become, the more you know; your bank account of knowledge is much richer."
~ William Holden ~

"I think all this talk about age is foolish. Every time I'm one year older, everyone else is too."
~ Gloria Swanson ~

"Do not grow old, no matter how long you live. Never cease to stand like curious children before the Great Mystery into which we were born."
~ Albert Einstein ~

"I'd like to be Dakota Fanning when I get young."
~ Jodie Foster ~

Audiences

"Never tell the audience how good you are; they will soon find that out for themselves."
~ *Harry Houdini* ~

"The man who tries to be funny is lost. To lose one's naturalness is always to lose the sympathy of your audience."
~ *Harold Lloyd* ~

"I always want the audience to out-guess me, and then I double-cross them."
~ *Buster Keaton* ~

"Nobody ever lost a dollar by underestimating the taste of the American public."
~ *P.T. Barnum* ~

"I think if you ask the audience to like you, it's all over."
~ *Rachel Weisz* ~

"I realized very quickly that the public has a perfect right to tell you what they want to see."
~ *Burt Reynolds* ~

"It proves what they say, give the public what they want to see and they'll come out for it."
~ *Red Skelton* ~

"If you give audiences a chance,
they'll do half your acting for you."
~ *Katharine Hepburn* ~

"When I'm on stage, I really think of it as: I'm there to serve you, and not myself. I don't think I've ever heard the applause."
~ *Jared Leto* ~

"Is it mere thespian paranoia to feel that everybody in the world wants to be an actor and secretly resents the lucky few who make it? Certainly, the audience in the theatre is not far from the audience in the Big Top watching the funambulist, thrilled by the risk he's taking, but unconsciously longing for him to fall. At the very least, the fact that he *might* fall is a large part of their enjoyment."
~ *Simon Callow* ~

"The audience is a dark thing, a peculiar animal, an enemy that must be assaulted and won. It doesn't matter a damn what the actor does or does not feel. It's what the lady down there in the blue hat is feeling."
~ *George C. Scott* ~

"I love the theater because I love the live audience and when we went three cameras we had a live audience in the study so we had someone to play to and react to. That laughter!"
~ *Jack Klugman* ~

"I'm really only happy when I'm on stage. I just feed off the energy of the audience. That's what I'm all about—people and laughter."
~ *Larry David* ~

"I am a real ham. I love an audience. I work better with an audience. I am dead, in fact, without one."
~ *Lucille Ball* ~

"I'd like to make you laugh for about ten minutes though I'm gonna be on for an hour."
~ *Richard Pryor* ~

"Audiences always sound like they're glad to see me, and I'm damned glad to see them."
~ *Claudette Colbert* ~

"The number of people who will not go to a show they do not want to see is unlimited."
~ *Oscar Hammerstein II* ~

"I'm not playing for other musicians. We're trying to reach the guy who works all day and wants to spend a buck at night. We'll keep him happy."
~ *Nat King Cole* ~

"I can think of nothing that an audience won't understand. The only problem is to interest them; once they are interested, they understand anything in the world."
~ *Orson Welles* ~

"There is more money in being liked by an audience than in being disliked by it. The biggest thing about movie audiences is the sympathy they give characters on the screen."
~ *William Powell* ~

"I can play a man who's despicable. But I'll still look inside him to find a point of connection. If I can find that kernel, audiences will relate to me."
~ *Forest Whitaker* ~

"If you are writing a story and trying to draw an audience to come and hear you tell it, it's got to in some way relate to them. Who wants to come and hear about your specific problems? It's not therapy. It's supposed to be a communal piece of entertainment."
~ *Matt Damon* ~

"I do miss the rhythms of comedy. And I've never been able to perform very well without an audience. The sitcoms I've done had them. It was like doing a little play."
~ *Dick Van Dyke* ~

"I look at myself as an audience member. I still love movies, and I still go and sit in the back of the big dark room with everybody else, and I want the same thrill."
~ *Samuel L. Jackson* ~

"Inside of all the makeup … it's you, and I think that's what the audience is really interested in … you, how you're going to cope with the situation, the obstacles, the troubles that the writer put in front of you."
~ *Gregory Peck* ~

"Never complain when the audience fails to applaud."
~ *Henning Nelms* ~

"As an actor to watch an audience of people howl together in a single mind as a result of work you've done together with friends is a privilege."
~ Tommy Lee Jones ~

"The truth is that everyone pays attention to who's number one at the box office. And none of it matters, because the only thing that really exists is the connection the audience has with a movie."
~ Tom Hanks ~

"Never treat your audience as customers, always as partners."
~ James Stewart ~

"I tend to believe that audiences are relatively well-balanced people."
~ Clint Eastwood ~

"An actor really is a kind of intermediary between an audience and the piece, whether it's a play or movie."
~ Christopher Walken ~

"There is a kind of invisible thread between the actor and the audience, and when it's there it's stunning, and there is nothing to match that."
~ Maggie Smith ~

"On stage I make love to twenty-five thousand people; then I go home alone."
~ Janis Joplin ~

Auditions

"There were years in between of going to auditions pretty much every day and getting nothing."
~ *Lucy Boynton* ~

"I went for endless auditions for tiny parts in obscure plays, and never got one job until I was in *Four Weddings*."
~ *Anna Chancellor* ~

"Unless you are an enormous name, you never stop auditioning."
~ *Richard E. Grant* ~

"I like to wear my dad's shoes to auditions as sort of a lucky thing. I feel like I'm on solid ground."
~ *Bill Pullman* ~

"It makes me believe in fate. In most cases, the readings where I've been really bad have usually been the ones where I got the part."
~ *Robin Wright* ~

"The greatest thing is that usually the auditions you think are bad are the ones you get."
~ *Lily James* ~

"Acting takes a lot of practice, but so does auditioning."
~ *Vincent Rodriguez III* ~

"The real trick to auditioning is just letting go of trying to please them. Make it your own. That took me a long time to learn."
~ Allison Janney ~

"I trained myself, whenever I walk into auditions, to hate everyone in the room."
~ Adam Driver ~

"When I was auditioning for drama school and looking for a monologue, it was all, 'I'm whining about my period or my baby that has died or my boyfriend …' Why can't you have a normal girl, talking about ideas?"
~ Vanessa Kirby ~

"Once you've gotten the job, there's nothing to it. If you're an actor, you're an actor. Doing it is not the hard part. The hard part is getting to do it."
~ Morgan Freeman ~

"I've had heartbreaking auditions where they don't even look at you. You're out before you're in."
~ Rachel McAdams ~

"I used to cry on the way to auditions."
~ Chyler Leigh ~

"Auditions are hard. You should see what most of the women look like when I audition for things—they look like they should be on the catwalk."
~ Mayim Bialik ~

"What's so kind of beautiful about the whole thing was that everything that made me not right for all of those hundreds of commercial auditions that I went on and no one ever wanted me for is what made me perfectly right for *Real Women Have Curves*."
~ America Ferrera ~

"I'm a natural blonde. But when I started acting, I would go to auditions and they didn't know where to put me because I was voluptuous and had the accent, but I had blonde hair. It was ignorance. They thought every Latin person looks like Salma Hayek."
~ Sofia Vergara ~

"People think that I can just walk into a room and get a job, but of the two hundred interviews and auditions I go through a year, I may get three yeses. I just have to use my sense of humor to get me through."
~ Oona Chaplin ~

"If you only live in the world of the actor, and if you only live in the world of auditions, etc., then you don't really have a whole lot to offer when it comes to playing the humans that you're trying to audition for."
~ Allison Tolman ~

"I have friends that are much better actors than I am that had to quit the business because they couldn't survive the auditions or the rejections, or people just didn't realize how good they were."
~ Robert Englund ~

"I always look at auditions as not even getting the job as much as I'm just trying to connect with this casting director so they remember me for next time."
~ *Sebastian Stan* ~

"You've got to think of things as an opportunity. An audition's an opportunity to have an audience."
~ *Al Pacino* ~

"I hate auditions. When I'm doing them, I can't wait to get out the bleeding door."
~ *Ian Hart* ~

"Now when I get auditions, I choose to believe that I am an amazing actor."
~ *Rachele Brooke Smith* ~

"My dad never told me that when you audition, you might not get the role. He wanted to wait until my first disappointment to tell me."
~ *Haley Joel Osment* ~

"Auditioning is extremely bizarre. Just being an actor is extremely bizarre, but I wouldn't have it any other way."
~ *Adelaide Kane* ~

"For me, I love auditioning."
~ *Josh Hutcherson* ~

Authenticity and Being Yourself

"Because we're actors we can pretend and fake it,
but I'd rather the intimate investment was authentic."
~ *Keanu Reeves* ~

"Actors, who should pride themselves on their singularity,
are forever trying to be someone else. It isn't necessary for you,
the actor, to like yourself—self-love isn't easy to come by for
most of us—but you must learn to trust who you are.
There is no one else like you."
~ *Michael Shurtleff* ~

"Be yourself; everyone else is already taken."
~ *Oscar Wilde* ~

"The only thing you can ever be in life is yourself because
that's the only thing someone else can't be."
~ *Kirstie Alley* ~

"Don't hide your scars. They make you who you are."
~ *Frank Sinatra* ~

"I can't live in comparison.
I don't know those people who died. I'm me."
~ *Stephanie Knights* ~

"The beaten path is the safest, but the traffic's terrible."
~ *Jeff Taylor* ~

"You're only given a little spark of madness.
If you lose that, you're nothing."
~ Robin Williams ~

"It does take a long time and a lot of paint
to become our own artist."
~ Kate Jackson ~

"It's just better to be yourself than to try to be some version
of what you think the other person wants."
~ Matt Damon ~

"It takes courage to grow up and turn out
to be who you really are."
~ e. e. cummings ~

"Do you want to know who you are? Don't ask. Act!
Action will delineate and define you."
~ Thomas Jefferson ~

"Be who you are and say what you feel, because those who
mind don't matter, and those who matter don't mind."
~ Bernard Baruch ~

"They laugh at me because I'm different.
I laugh at them because they're all the same."
~ Kurt Cobain ~

"You are unique, and if that is not fulfilled,
then something has been lost."
~ Martha Graham ~

Awards

"At the Golden Globes, they put all the bigger stars in the front; the movie stars in the front, TV actors in the back. But even as a movie star, you can be outseated by a bigger star in any given year. It's kind of hilarious. You have to take it in stride."
~ Julianne Moore ~

"Do awards change careers? Well, I haven't heard of many stories where that's the case. It's a fun excuse to meet colleagues and celebrate people who've done well that year in certain people's eyes, and it's nothing more than that."
*~ **Benedict Cumberbatch** ~*

"Awards for arts, where you make comparisons, don't make much sense."
*~ **Viggo Mortensen** ~*

"Awards are meaningless for actors, unless they all play the same part."
*~ **Humphrey Bogart** ~*

"Now, there are so many movies, so many festivals, and so many awards going on, each judged with each other, like your work is worse than others and that's not fair. How can you tell what's best and what's worst from these awards? We're talking about art."
~ Javier Bardem ~

"I've always found it embarrassing to receive awards."
~ Sam Shepard ~

"People think you know beforehand when you win an Oscar—I can assure you you don't."
~ Judi Dench ~

"The Oscar sits on some shelf above my desk. If there was an earthquake, I could actually be killed by my own Academy Award."
~ Helen Hunt ~

"I see the Oscar in my bedroom, and it's like I bought it in a souvenir shop on Hollywood Boulevard."
~ Renée Zellweger ~

"My friend Quincy Jones says we won our first Grammys together in 1963. I have no recollection. I don't even remember the room. When he showed me the picture, I remembered what I wore. But it's like awards don't mean anything."
~ Barbra Streisand ~

"I don't deserve this award, but I have arthritis and I don't deserve that either."
~ Jack Benny ~

"Awards are so unnecessary because I think we get so much out of our work just by doing it. The work is a reward in itself.
~ Natalie Portman ~

"I had a friend who worked at a hospice, and he said people in their final moments don't discuss their successes, awards or what books they wrote or what they accomplished. They only talk about their loves and their regrets, and I think that's very telling."
~ Brad Pitt ~

"Don't work for recognition, but do work worthy of recognition."
~ H. Jackson Browne ~

"Awards are meaningless to me, and I have nothing but disdain for anyone who actively campaigns to get one."
~ Bill Murray ~

"I love awards, especially if I get them."
~ Ben Gazzara ~

"Awards sell tickets and they're a clever publicity stunt."
~ Tony Randall ~

"Trophies and medals have never meant much to me. I've had amazing experiences, which let you feel like you've accomplished something."
~ John Krasinski ~

"I feel very blessed to have two wonderful, healthy children who keep me completely grounded, sane and throw up on my shoes just before I go to an awards show just so I know to keep it real."
~ Reese Witherspoon ~

Awareness

"I was always an observer, even as a child. I could be satisfied to sit in a car for three hours and just look at the street go by while my mother went shopping."
~ Jonathan Winters ~

"I had a dream I was awake and I woke up to find myself asleep."
~ Stan Laurel ~

"To be an artist means never to avert one's eyes."
~ Akira Kurosawa ~

"Observancy is a dying art."
~ Stanley Kubrick ~

"There is one thing we can do, and the happiest people are those who do it to the limit of their ability. We can be completely present. We can be all here. We can … give all our attention to the opportunity before us."
~ Mark Van Doren ~

"When people talk, listen completely. Most people never listen."
~ Ernest Hemingway ~

"All I want to see from an actor is the intensity and accuracy of their listening."
~ Alan Rickman ~

"What I do for a living is listen."
~ Val Kilmer ~

"You can't fake listening."
~ Raquel Welch ~

"Nobody sees a flower, really—it is so small we haven't time, and to see takes time."
~ Georgia O'Keefe ~

"If we could see the miracle of a single flower clearly, our whole life would change."
~ Buddha ~

"Everything has beauty, but not everyone sees it."
~ Confucius ~

"Everything that is made beautiful and fair and lovely is made for the eyes of one who sees."
~ Rumi ~

"One never notices what has been done; one can only see what remains to be done."
~ Marie Curie ~

"Our task is not to change our life-scenery, but to lift the mental fog that distorts its charm."
~ Vernon Howard ~

"The awareness of our own strength makes us modest."
~ Paul Cezanne ~

Beauty

"No one ever told me I was pretty when I was a little girl. All little girls should be told they're pretty, even if they aren't."
~ Marilyn Monroe ~

"I thought Marilyn Monroe was the most beautiful woman in the world and Elizabeth Taylor breathtaking. But, when I see myself on the screen, I say: 'Oh shoot! What are they talking about?'"
~ Farrah Fawcett ~

"I don't spend a lot of time in the mirror."
~ Julia Roberts ~

"Growing up, I was the plain one. I had no style. I was the tough kid with the comb in the back pocket and the feathered hair."
~ Cameron Diaz ~

"I am definitely not the best-looking. I did not grow up feeling like I was particularly attractive. You should have seen me at fourteen, with braces and glasses, gangly and doing ballet! If I looked good in *Wolf of Wall Street*, I cannot take full credit. It was because of hair extensions and makeup."
~ Margot Robbie ~

"I suffered from 'No one will ever fancy me!' syndrome well into my teens. Even now, I do not consider myself to be some kind of great, sexy beauty. Absolutely not."
~ Kate Winslet ~

"I was very flattered by the sex-kitten thing because
I never thought of myself as that."
~ Ann-Margret ~

"Being a sex symbol was rather like being a convict.
The mind is an erogenous zone."
~ Raquel Welch ~

"I don't have sex appeal and I know it. As a matter of fact,
I think I'm rather funny looking. My teeth are funny, for one
thing, and I have none of the attributes usually required
for a movie queen, including the shapeliness."
~ Audrey Hepburn ~

"I had ordered long legs, but they never arrived.
My eyes are weird too, one is gray and the other is green.
I have a crooked smile and my nose looks like a ski slope.
No, I would not win a Miss contest."
~ Jane Seymour ~

"I always thought I had crooked eyebrows and crooked teeth.
That's why I never understood why people called me a beauty."
~ Lauren Bacall ~

"Tall, sandy blonde, with sort of blue eyes, skinny in places,
fat in others. An average gal."
~ Uma Thurman ~

"Beauty is not just physical."
~ Halle Berry ~

"It's how you look at beauty. Is it only an outward appearance with hair and makeup and a hot body, or is it something deeper than that?"
~ *Hilary Swank* ~

"I don't know who decided that skinny was more appealing than not skinny. It seems arbitrary."
~ *Gwyneth Paltrow* ~

"Feeling beautiful has nothing to do with what you look like. I promise."
~ *Emma Watson* ~

"I never looked like an ingenue. I don't want to be America's sweetheart; I'd rather be something they don't quite understand."
~ *Tammy Grimes* ~

"I spent many nights crying myself to sleep wishing I was ugly because of the way men leered and disrespected me, because they assumed things about my mental capacity or my physical willingness based on the way I look."
~ *Evangeline Lilly* ~

"I'm never going to starve myself for a part. I'm invincible. I don't want little girls to be like, 'Oh, I want to look like Katniss, so I'm going to skip dinner!'"
~ *Jennifer Lawrence* ~

"Beauty is in all shapes and sizes."
~ *Holland Roden* ~

"The trouble with beauty is that it's like being
born rich and getting poorer."
~ Joan Collins ~

"Character contributes to beauty.
It fortifies a woman as her youth fades."
~ Jacqueline Bisset ~

"I simply did not want my face to be my talent."
~ Gene Tierney ~

"Building on beauty … seems to me the
worst thing any girl can do."
~ Thelma Todd ~

"Hollywood sold its stars on good looks and personality build-ups.
We weren't really actresses in the true sense. We were just big
names—the products of a good publicity department.
Today's crop of actresses and actors have real talent.
Good looks are no longer an essential part of the business."
~ Ann Southern ~

"We all have a weakness for beauty."
~Albert Camus ~

"Beauty is a horrible power."
~ Faina Ranevskaya ~

"Beauty awakens the soul to act."
~ Dante Alighieri ~

Believing

"It's not what is available or unavailable that determines your level of success and happiness; it's what you convince yourself is true."
~ Dr. Wayne Dyer ~

"Believe in yourself; you may succeed when others do not believe in you, but never when you do not believe in yourself."
~ Orison Swett Marden ~

"Believe. No pessimist ever discovered the secrets of the stars, or sailed to an uncharted island, or opened a new heaven to the human spirit."
~ Helen Keller ~

"He does not believe who does not live according to his belief."
~ Thomas Fuller ~

"Belief is like a thermostat that regulates what we accomplish in life."
~ David J. Schwartz ~

"Your belief determines your action and your action determines your results, but first you have to believe."
~ Mark Victor Hansen ~

"Whatever your mind believes, your body will manifest."
~ Olivia Fox Cabane ~

"Always think of what you have to do as easy and it will become so."
~ Emile Coue ~

"Don't think. Believe. Trust your heart, not your brain. Don't think. Feel. Believe."
~ Ayn Rand ~

"In order to be a realist, you must believe in miracles."
~ David Ben Gurion ~

"Anyone who does not believe in miracles is not a realist."
~ Audrey Hepburn ~

"If you believe you can, you probably can. If you believe you won't, you most assuredly won't. Belief is the ignition switch that gets you off the launching pad."
~ Denis Waitley ~

"You will act like the sort of person you conceive yourself to be."
~ Maxwell Maltz ~

"Believe you can and you're halfway there."
~ Theodore Roosevelt ~

"As long as you have life and breath, believe."
~ Mark Helprin ~

"I never think of losing."
~ Lou Ferrigno ~

Circumstances

"Our experience of many life circumstances is a function of our personal perspective and not the circumstance itself."
~ Lindsay Wagner ~

"People are always blaming their circumstances for what they are. I don't believe in circumstances. The people who get on in this world are the people who get up and look for the circumstances they want, and—if they can't find them—make them."
~ George Bernard Shaw ~

"Man is not the creature of circumstances, circumstances are the creatures of men. We are free agents, and man is more powerful than matter."
~ Benjamin Disraeli ~

"The truth is that the only aspect of life you have any control over is your own reaction to the events taking place."
~ Dr. Richard Carlson ~

"Everything that happens to you can work for your good if you let it."
~ Tyler Perry ~

"As an actor, the toughest thing is being subject to circumstance. Meaning: 'What scripts are out there that are available?'"
~ Paul Dano ~

"Successful people make the most of the best
and the best of the worst."
~ *Steve Keating* ~

"Things turn out best for the people who make
the best of the way things work out."
~ *Art Linkletter* ~

"Could it be that we allow the conditions in our lives
to distract us from the meaning of our lives?"
~ *T. D. Jakes* ~

"It is not what happens to you that determines how far you
go in life; it is what you do with what happens to you."
~ *Zig Ziglar* ~

"Either you are creating your life or the circumstances are."
~ *Thomas Leonard* ~

"Your present circumstances don't determine where you can go;
they merely determine where you start."
~ *Nido Qubein* ~

"Do not let circumstances control you.
You change your circumstances."
~ *Jackie Chan* ~

"Circumstances, hell! I make circumstances!"
~ *Bruce Lee* ~

Comedy

"I have no agenda except to be funny. Neither I or the writers profess to offer any worldly wisdom."
~ Julia Louis-Dreyfus ~

"You can give a guy a funny line, but you can't make him say it funny."
~ Brad Garrett ~

"No one wants to say, 'That's not funny,' when you're working."
~ Bill Pullman ~

"To be a comedian you have to get onstage and find out if you're funny."
~ Rodney Dangerfield ~

"I don't think you can teach people how to be funny. You can make suggestions about how to speak a line or get a laugh, but it has to be in them."
~ George Cukor ~

"I enjoy comedic things. People don't understand it's the hardest thing to do. We have a ratio of twenty-five-to-one between good dramatic actors and people who are considered good comic actors."
~ Charles Grodin ~

"Comedy is hard to do. All the clichés about it are true."
~ Jeff Daniels ~

"Comedy is much harder, it's a lot more exacting. You can't just be real and you can't just use the same kind of techniques you use to fill up a regular scene."
~ *Jack Nicholson* ~

"There's something dangerous about what's funny. Jarring and disconcerting. There is a connection between funny and scary."
~ *Christopher Walken* ~

"A comedian does funny things. A good comedian does things funny."
~ *Buster Keaton* ~

"The more trouble you get a man into, the more comedy you get out of him.'"
~ *Harold Lloyd* ~

"Harold Lloyd was not a comedian. But he was the finest actor to play a comedian that I ever saw."
~ *Hal Roach* ~

"The more Keystone comedies I make, the more convinced I become that comedy is an art, and a high one at that. If those who are inclined to scoff at me will try their hand at directing just one of those comedies they designate as anything but art, I am pretty certain they will concede me my point."
~ *Mack Sennett* ~

"Silences are the most underrated part of comedy."
~ *David Steinberg* ~

"I really can't be funny unless it's part of the character. It really bugs me when someone thinks of me as a comic. If I read 'comedian Jack Lemmon,' I gag. That means I'm not an actor—which I am."
~ Jack Lemmon ~

"One of the biggest misconceptions about me is that I'm a comedian, which I'm not. A comedian is someone who can stand up in front of an audience and make you laugh. I've never done stand-up and I never will. I'm a comic actor. My comedy comes through my characters."
~ Eugene Levy ~

"I'm a classic example of all humorists—only funny when I'm working."
~ Peter Sellers ~

"Someone who makes you laugh is a comedian. Someone who makes you think and then laugh is a humorist."
~ George Burns ~

"The trouble with most comedians who try to do satire is that they are essentially brash, noisy and indelicate people who have to use a sledge hammer to smash a butterfly."
~ Imogene Coca ~

"Sight gags had to be planned; they required timing and mechanics. Occasionally, spontaneity would arise in the shooting of the scenes."
~ Stan Laurel ~

"When I get some budding young comic who'll come up to me and say, 'What was it like to do it in those days?' I try to be as gracious to him as Stan Laurel was to me."
~ *Dick Van Dyke* ~

"Being a funny person does an awful lot of things to you. You feel you musn't get serious with people. They don't expect it from you and they don't want to see it. You're not entitled to be serious, you're a clown."
~ *Fanny Brice* ~

"I wanted to make a living, but I really was not interested in money at all. I was interested in being a great comedian."
~ *Larry David* ~

"Success is the enemy of comedy."
~ *Jerry Seinfeld* ~

"The best way to ruin a comedy is to throw a lot of money at it."
~ *Jay Leno* ~

"When the kids are laughing in the audience, I tear up, I'm so happy I did a nice thing."
~ *Adam Sandler* ~

"Comedy was my sport. It taught me how to roll with the punches. Failure is the exact same as success when it comes to comedy because it just keeps coming. It never stops."
~ *Emma Stone* ~

"Comedy itself is based upon very old principles of which I can readily name seven. They are, in short: the joke, exaggeration, ridicule, ignorance, surprise, the pun, and finally, the comic situation."
~ Jack Benny ~

"There's a thin line between to laugh with and to laugh at."
~ Richard Pryor ~

"If I can get you to laugh with me, you like me better, which makes you more open to my ideas. And if I can persuade you to laugh at the particular point I make, by laughing at it you acknowledge its truth."
~ John Cleese ~

"Comedy has to be based on truth. You take the truth and you put a little curlicue at the end."
~ Sid Caesar ~

"The absolute truth is the thing that makes people laugh."
~ Carl Reiner ~

"You don't necessarily have to be a funny person to get a laugh."
~ Lucille Ball ~

"Comedy equals tragedy plus time."
~ Carol Burnett ~

"Comedy is merely tragedy happening to someone else."
~ W. C. Fields ~

Complacency and Comfort Zones

"I write with my left hand even though I'm right-handed, I walk backwards in a very safe place—anything that engages your brain."
~ *Rita Moreno* ~

"With everything I work on, I want to be put in a position that I have to be brave to do the project."
~ *Maggie Gyllenhaal* ~

"I say, 'Be brave. Do it even if your ankles shake, because they will.'"
~ *Rose McGowan* ~

"We go through life trying to seek security and not coming outside of our comfort zones, and we take most of our stuff with us to the grave."
~ *Les Brown* ~

"I think actors get too comfortable. I like being uncomfortable as an actor because it keeps you alive. I don't know, I think it's important."
~ *Peter Dinklage* ~

"We are called upon to do something new, to confront a no man's land, to push into a forest where there are no well-worn paths and from which no one has returned to guide us."
~ *Rollo May* ~

"Behold the turtle: He only makes progress when
he sticks his neck out."
~ James Bryant Conant ~

"Discomfort is the price of admission to a meaningful life."
~ Susan David ~

"Comfort zones are most often expanded through discomfort."
~ Peter McWilliams ~

"I feel that people need to be jolted out of their comfort zones."
~ Saul Williams ~

"Our comfort zones can be our greatest enemy to our potential."
~ David Cottrell ~

"Comfort zones are overrated. They make you lazy."
~ Melina Marchetta ~

"The best things in life are often waiting for you
at the exit ramp of your comfort zone."
~ Karen Salmansohn ~

"Safety and comfort comes with complacency,
and that's never a good place to be working from."
~ Elijah Wood ~

"You have to leave the city of your comfort and go into
the wilderness of your intuition. What you'll discover
will be wonderful. What you'll discover is yourself."
~ Alan Alda ~

Contribution

"I am a great believer in what we've been told time and time again by people like Joseph Campbell, 'find your bliss.' Find out what it is that touches you most deeply. Pursue it, learn about it, explore it, expand on it. Live with it and nurture it. Find your own way and make your own contribution. Find a way to make a contribution to this society because God knows we need contributions from the coming generation. This planet and this civilization is in need. I see it as a time of need."
~ *Leonard Nimoy* ~

"When we quit thinking primarily about ourselves and our own self-preservation, we undergo a truly heroic transformation of consciousness."
~ *Joseph Murphy* ~

"It's important for me to try my hand at philanthropy because I want to leave behind a record of someone who did more than just gobble up stuff for themselves. I realized that a life lived for yourself is not much of a life."
~ *Ben Affleck* ~

"If you can't help people, then what is the point of being successful?"
~ *Matt Damon* ~

"The sole meaning of life is to serve humanity"
~ *Leo Tolstoy* ~

"How wonderful it is that nobody need wait a single moment before starting to improve the world."
~ *Anne Frank* ~

"It has been written that a useless life is far worse than an early death."
~ *Og Mandino* ~

"Be ashamed to die until you have won some victory for humanity."
~ *Horace Mann* ~

"Take part. Contribute. Be interested in everything and everybody."
~ *Claude Rains* ~

"When I give, I give myself."
~ *Walt Whitman* ~

"Only those who have learned the power of sincere and selfless contribution experience life's deepest joy: true fulfillment."
~ *Anthony Robbins* ~

"I don't know what your destiny will be, but one thing I know: the only ones among you who will be really happy are those who will have sought and found how to serve."
~ *Albert Schweitzer* ~

"Get busy with life's purpose, toss aside empty hopes. Get active in your own rescue."
~ *Marcus Aurelius* ~

Creativity

"Bring ideas in and entertain them royally,
for one of them may be the king."
~ Mark Van Doren ~

"The best ideas come as jokes.
Make your thinking as funny as possible."
~ David Ogilvy ~

"All creative people want to do the unexpected."
~ Hedy Lamarr ~

"Never cry over spilled milk. Find a use for it.
Or invent a better milk carton."
~ Jack Foster ~

"Creativity involves breaking out of established patterns
in order to look at things in a different way."
~ Edward de Bono ~

"Creativity takes courage."
~ Henri Matisse ~

"You can't use up creativity.
The more you use, the more you have."
~ Maya Angelou ~

"Creativity is making the complicated simple."
~ Charles Mingus ~

"Don't think about making art, just get it done. Let everyone else decide if it's good or bad, whether they love it or hate it. While they are deciding, make even more art."
~ Andy Warhol ~

"The most creative people have this childlike facility to play."
~ John Cleese ~

"If you are willing to do something that might not work, you're closer to being an artist."
~ Seth Godin ~

"An essential aspect of creativity is not being afraid to fail."
~ Edwin Land ~

"Creativity is not the finding of a thing, but the making something out of it after it is found."
~ James Russell Lowell ~

"Creative isn't the way I think. It's the way I live."
~ Paul Sandip ~

"Everyone is a genius at least once a year; a real genius has his original ideas closer together."
~ George C. Lichtenberg ~

"Creativity is a habit, and the best creativity is the result of good work habits."
~ Twyla Tharp ~

"Creativity is what helps me escape a lot of my inner demons."
~ Demi Lovato ~

Criticism

"I never met anybody who said when they were a kid,
I wanna grow up and be a critic."
~ *Richard Pryor* ~

"To be honest with you, when I got into this I never thought about reviews. I never thought about what people would say about me. I was just a young guy who was excited to become a comedian and an actor and I just wanted
to get to do what I got to do."
~ *Adam Sandler* ~

"The reviewer is a singularly detested enemy because he is,
unlike the hapless artist, invulnerable."
~ *Carroll O'Connor* ~

"Actually, I am a golfer. That is my real occupation.
I never was an actor. Ask anybody, particularly the critics."
~ *Victor Mature* ~

"Critics don't buy records. They get 'em free."
~ *Nat King Cole* ~

"A successful man is one who can lay a firm foundation
with the bricks others have thrown at him."
~ *David Brinkley* ~

"Bad reviews I've gotten never diminished the number of people in my audience; good reviews have never added to the number of people in my audience; be your own critic."
~ Frank Sinatra ~

"The critics had an image of me, and they wouldn't accept any other ... I was a cartoon character. A joke."
~ Ann-Margret ~

"There's a lot of judgment that can come from outside sometimes, and there's media scrutiny that is placed on a lot of women in the public eye, and I just couldn't care less. I really couldn't care less."
~ Kate Winslet ~

"You already feel unsure of yourself, and then you see your worst fears in print. It really knocked me—which is why, I think, I was working, working, working, because I was trying to run away from the fact that I thought I couldn't do it."
~ Keira Knightley ~

"If people don't like your work, all the still pictures in the world can't help you and nothing written about you, even oceans of it, will make you popular."
~ Jean Arthur ~

"Honest criticism is hard to take, particularly from a relative, a friend, an acquaintance, or a stranger."
~ Franklin P. Jones ~

"Every actor in his heart believes everything bad that's printed about him."
~ *Orson Welles* ~

"Write anything you want about me. Make up something. Hell, I don't care."
~ *Spencer Tracy* ~

"If you focus on doing the work, you'll get to a place of refinement where those reviews which are often hyped up too much to the negative or the positive fall away."
~ *Robert Redford* ~

"I, along with the critics, have never taken myself very seriously."
~ *Elizabeth Taylor* ~

"You have been criticizing yourself for years and it hasn't worked. Try approving of yourself and see what happens."
~ *Louise L. Hay* ~

"Do what you feel in your heart to be right—for you'll be criticized anyway."
~ *Eleanor Roosevelt* ~

"The only difference between criticism and feedback is how you take it."
~ *Tim Grover* ~

"The bad reviews get to me, believe me."
~ *Daniel Craig* ~

Decisions

"It is in your moments of decision that your destiny is shaped."
~ Anthony Robbins ~

"I have several times made a poor choice by avoiding
a necessary confrontation."
~ John Cleese ~

"In any moment of decision, the best thing you can do is
the right thing, the next best thing is the wrong thing,
and the worst thing you can do is nothing."
~ Theodore Roosevelt ~

"I'm happy about the things I've done. Not always happy about the results, but happy about the decisions, because I made them myself. And I think that's an important way to go through life."
~ Kevin Costner ~

"The worst thing one can do is not to try, to be aware
of what one wants and not give in to it, to spend years
in silent hurt wondering if something could have
materialized—never knowing."
~ Jim Rohn ~

"You always have options. You may just not like those options."
~ Tim Ferriss ~

"Pick battles big enough to matter, small enough to win."
~ Jonathan Kozel ~

"If it's anything I can't stand it's yes-men. When I say no, I want you to say no, too."
~ Jack Warner ~

"I don't want yes-men around me. I want everyone to tell the truth, even if it costs them their jobs."
~ Samuel Goldwyn ~

"In any moment of decision, the best thing you can do is the right thing, the next best thing is the wrong thing, and the worst thing you can do is nothing."
~ Theodore Roosevelt ~

"People make troubles for themselves. No one forces them to choose boring jobs, marry the wrong person, or buy uncomfortable shoes."
~ Faina Ranevskaya ~

"No trumpets sound when the important decisions of our life are made. Destiny is made known silently."
~ Agnes de Mille ~

"Tough times call for tougher decisions."
~ Prabhas ~

"Decisions are made by those who show up."
~ Aaron Sorkin ~

Depression

"Depression is a prison where you are both the
suffering prisoner and the cruel jailer."
~ *Dorothy Rowe* ~

"Despair is a narcotic. It lulls the mind into indifference."
~ *Charlie Chaplin* ~

"If you only walk on sunny days,
you'll never reach your destination."
~ *Paulo Coelho* ~

"You need to know what to do when the sun is not shining."
~ *Robert Downey Jr.* ~

"I was fine when it came to cheering up others,
not so fine with myself."
~ *Gene Tierney* ~

"I think the saddest people always try their hardest to make
people happy because they know what it's like to feel absolutely
worthless and they don't want anyone else to feel like that."
~ *Robin Williams* ~

"The artist's job is not to succumb to despair, but to find
an antidote for the emptiness of existence."
~ *Woody Allen* ~

"I was a sullen kid who smoked cigarettes and wore black every day, and I went to a school that was lacrosse players and Izods."
~ *Peter Dinklage* ~

"You have to remember there are tremendous chasms between the peaks. I've lost my grip before and it could happen again. It's a long way down and it gets deeper every time."
~ *Lee Marvin* ~

"It's very easy to go down, so always live up. Incline yourself upward."
~ *Jack Nicholson* ~

"Depression is being colorblind and constantly told how colorful the world is."
~ *Atticus* ~

"Even among familiar faces, people often feel invisible and desolate, like an island in cold waters or a shadow apart from the crowd. Be the reason another never feels alone."
~ *Richelle E. Goodrich* ~

"I found that with depression, one of the most important things you could realize is that you're not alone."
~ *Dwayne Johnson* ~

"Being in good physical shape is the best way to combat depression. You just have endorphins running around your body. It is the best anti-depressive that there is."
~ *Chris Pratt* ~

Discipline, Consistency, and Preparation

"I assault life. I decided a long time ago that it's like a game of basketball. Just assault it. Discipline is everything."
~ Robert James Waller ~

"The Marines gave me discipline I could live with. By the time I got out I could deal with things on a more realistic level. All in all, despite my problems, I liked my time in the Marines."
~ Steve McQueen ~

"I do not believe I could have built FedEx without the skills I learned from the Marine Corps."
~ Fred Smith ~

"We must all suffer one of two things: the pain of discipline or the pain of regret or disappointment."
~ Jim Rohn ~

"We don't have to be smarter than the rest. We have to be more disciplined than the rest."
~ Warren Buffet ~

"I was an okay boxer, I wasn't great, I was okay, but I loved the discipline of getting together every Monday, Wednesday and Friday, usually Saturday afternoons too, with a whole bunch of mates and training, very, very hard for about two and a half hours."
~ Liam Neeson ~

"The first thing you got to do if you want to be a fighter is to fight. I figured out once that by the time I got into the amateurs, I'd already had a thousand fights."
~ Jake LaMotta ~

"I fear not the man who has practiced ten thousand kicks once, but I fear the man who has practiced one kick ten thousand times."
~ Bruce Lee ~

"I don't do anything the same every day. Discipline is tough for a guy who is a rebel."
~ Jonathan Winters ~

"If you can't get out of something, get into it."
~ Kris Kristofferson ~

"The happily ever after comes after you've done the work."
~ Viola Davis ~

"We need to understand the difference between discipline and punishment. Punishment is what you do to someone; discipline is what you do for someone."
~ Zig Ziglar ~

"Discipline is the bridge between goals and accomplishment."
~ Jim Rohn ~

"If you're going through hell, keep going."
~ Winston Churchill ~

Doubts

"Our doubts are traitors and make us lose the good
we oft might win by fearing to attempt."
~ William Shakespeare ~

"Doubt, not self-reflection, comes from a destructive energy,
and when it rears its head, I talk to it like a lunatic."
~ Gwyneth Paltrow ~

"The degree to which people regularly underestimate
their capacity for accomplishment is immeasurable."
~ Earl Nightingale ~

"I doubt myself a lot but go forward at full throttle anyway."
~ Vanessa Kirby ~

"The only thing standing between me and greatness is me."
~ Woody Allen ~

"If you hear a voice within you say 'you cannot paint,'
then by all means paint, and that voice will be silenced."
~ Vincent van Gogh ~

"I don't believe anyone ever suspects how completely unsure
I am of my work and myself and what tortures of self-doubting
the doubt of others has always given me."
~ Tennessee Williams ~

"I don't think there's any artist of any value
who doesn't doubt what they're doing."
~ *Francis Ford Coppola* ~

"Every actor is full of doubts about himself, and I'm no exception. If you see those fears in yourself—and expose them—the audience can associate with you more deeply than if you try to play it safe and pretend to be the invincible tough guy. To show my strength is nothing; to show my weakness is everything. I suppose it takes a certain kind of strength to admit your fears, but I really don't think it's anything more than simple honesty."
~ *Lee Marvin* ~

"There were a lot of times I wondered if I was deluding myself. I had nothing else to fall back on, but I never enjoyed anything else."
~ *Edie Falco* ~

"To accomplish more, redirect your mental energy by continuously reminding yourself of all the things you do right."
~ *Brian Koslow* ~

"I was regarded as the school freak which further reinforced a lot of inhibitions and doubts I had about myself. I was a shy, frightened teenager for a long time.
~ *Winona Ryder* ~

"When you doubt your powers, you power your doubts."
~ *Brian Oldfield* ~

Drama

"Drama is life with the dull bits cut out."
~ Alfred Hitchcock ~

"A talent for drama is not a talent for writing, but is an ability to articulate human relationships."
~ Gore Vidal ~

"I made mistakes in drama. I thought drama was when actors cried. But drama is when the audience cries."
~ Frank Capra ~

"An actor entering through the door, you've got nothing. But if he enters through the window, you've got a situation."
~ Billy Wilder ~

"It's the exceptions that an actor should choose. It's what is exceptional that makes drama interesting, not everyday reality."
~ Michael Shurtleff ~

"I wanted to be a tragedienne. I only wanted sad parts. When mother read the press notices when I was on the road, saying I was a 'comedienne', the tears rolled down my cheeks. I thought comedians had to have black on their faces or red beards."
~ Dorothy Gish ~

"Drama starts where logic ends."
~ Ram Charan ~

"Drama lies in extreme exaggeration of the feelings,
an exaggeration that dislocates flat everyday reality."
~ *Eugene Ionesco* ~

"The unencumbered stage encourages the truth operative
in everyone. The less seen, the more heard. The eye is
the enemy of the ear in real drama."
~ *Thornton Wilder* ~

"I find myself gravitating towards drama. It interests me. In the
books I read, the paintings I like, it's always the darker stuff."
~ *Naomi Watts* ~

"I like taking a path into new country, and I always take the
darker path. Not because it's dark, but because there's a secret
there that you can share when you get out. That's what I liked
as a kid. That's how I approach my work. With a face like mine,
it's lucky I have a heart that likes that."
~ *Amanda Plummer* ~

"When a character is born, he acquires at once such an
independence, even of his own author, that he can be imagined
by everybody even in many other situations where the author
never dreamed of placing him; and so he acquires for himself
a meaning which the author never thought of giving him."
~ *Luigi Pirandello* ~

"Doing drama is, in a sense, easier. In doing comedy,
if you don't get that laugh, there's something wrong."
~ *Betty White* ~

Dreams

"If anyone has a dream out there, just know that I'm living proof that they do come true."
~ *Kim Basinger* ~

"My life has far exceeded what I might ever have dreamed of because I would never have been so bold as to dream that these things might happen to me."
~ *Renée Zellweger* ~

"My mom always told me I could do or be anything I dared to dream, and I always wanted to work in the movie industry."
~ *Octavia Spencer* ~

"I don't know what I did in this life to deserve all of this. I'm just a girl from a trailer park who had a dream."
~ *Hilary Swank* ~

"Dreams never hurt anybody if he keeps working right behind the dream to make as much of it come real as he can."
~ *F.W. Woolworth* ~

"Every great dream begins with a dreamer."
~ *Harriet Tubman* ~

"Dreams are sent by God."
~ *Homer* ~

"I used to think as I looked out on the Hollywood night, 'There must be thousands of girls sitting alone like me dreaming of being a movie star.' But I'm not going to worry about them. I'm dreaming the hardest."
~ Marilyn Monroe ~

"Rose-colored glasses are never made in bifocals. Nobody wants to read the small print in dreams."
~ Ann Landers ~

"What do dreams know of boundaries?"
~ Hilary Swank ~

"If a little dreaming is dangerous, the cure for it is not to dream less but to dream more, to dream all the time."
~ Marcel Proust ~

"Go confidently in the direction of your dreams. Live the life you have imagined."
~ Henry David Thoreau ~

"Neglected dreams become regrets."
~ Stephen Richards ~

"Believe in your dreams and dream big. And after you've done that, dream bigger."
~ Howard Schultz ~

"Dreams cost nothing. They're free."
~ Sylvester Stallone ~

Early Work

"I don't get bothered about statistics. If somebody had pointed out to me the odds of my being a working actress getting paid for what she does, I probably would have quit early in the game."
~ Shelley Long ~

"You know, the period of World War I and the Roaring Twenties were really just about the same as today. You worked, and you made a living if you could, and you tried to make the best of things. For an actor or a dancer, it was no different than today. It was a struggle."
~ James Cagney ~

"Yes, I'm blonde. When I started as an actor, because of the accent and my body and my personality, it was not what the stereotype of the Latina woman in Hollywood is, so they didn't know where to put me. The blond hair wasn't matching. The moment I put my hair dark, it was better for my work."
~ Sofia Vergara ~

"It's kind of heartbreaking when I talk about it now, I still get very moved by the lack of opportunities that were available to myself and to the very few others who were Hispanic young actresses."
~ Rita Moreno ~

"I wanted to do film. I was living in New York and working in theater, but I always wanted to do film."
~ Christopher Lloyd ~

"I was in Woody Allen's *Stardust Memories* in 1980. It was only a bit part and I didn't get to speak, but I felt that I was in a real movie and heading where I had always wanted to be."
~ Sharon Stone ~

"I acted when I was young, but at nineteen, I had my own theater company where I acted but also directed. I also did some theater in Los Angeles. So I was always wanting to direct, even before I became an established actor."
~ Rob Reiner ~

"I don't know why people think child actresses in particular are screwed up. I see kids everywhere who are totally bored. I've never been bored a day in my life."
~ Jodie Foster ~

"I started singing at the Met when I was seven, and the competition was so fierce that it really prepared me."
~ Emmy Rossum ~

"Even in elementary school, I took it really seriously. I was always doing plays."
~ Maggie Gyllenhaal ~

"I began acting when River was doing this TV series and they needed two kids for the show, so they got me and my little sister, Summer, to do it. After that I did some really weird guest spots with orangutans and stuff."
~ Joaquin Phoenix ~

"I grew up in the world of bad television, on my dad's sets and then as a young schmuck on dating shows and so on."
~ George Clooney ~

"When I got cast in *Rocky IV*, I had never seen a film camera before. And here I was in this boxing movie."
~ Dolph Lundgren ~

"I'd played dumbasses a lot. On *Mad About You*, I played a very dumb waitress and they saw me."
~ Lisa Kudrow ~

"I didn't get my first pilot that I screen-tested for, and I really thought it was the end of the world. But it's fine, you know, you move on to something else."
~ Rachel McAdams ~

"I can remember crying on the set of *Beverly Hills 90210* after being released from the show a few years ago."
~ Hilary Swank ~

"I probably worked every single entertainment medium, including some that don't exist. I worked the circus, carnival, I had my own medicine show, I worked eighteen years of radio."
~ Al Lewis ~

"From 1932 through 1934, I'd only worked three months. Every play I got into folded."
~ James Stewart ~

"I was in the business ten years before the actors began to notice me. Then it took another five years before the agents and producers noticed me. Five years after that, the public found me. And five or six years later, the critics took note."
~ *Charles Durning* ~

"I only took acting lessons because my whole thing, really, was to direct. But my first jobs were acting jobs."
~ *James Coburn* ~

"I remember that I used to get on the phone with Ellen Barkin. We were both unemployed. Nobody would hire us. For every part that we wanted, Debra Winger would steal. We could not get a job and we'd be hysterical for hours on the phone, bitching and moaning and kvetching."
~ *Michelle Pfeiffer* ~

"John Lennon and Ringo Starr liked my songs. I used to write songs and they heard me sing songs on stage in London."
~ *Ben Kingsley* ~

"I think every American actor wants to be a movie star. But I never wanted to do stupid movies. I wanted to do films. I vowed I would never do a commercial or a soap opera—both of which I did as soon as I left the Acting Company and was starving."
~ *Kevin Kline* ~

"The Lord Chamberlin was censoring scripts when I first came into the theater."
~ *Judi Dench* ~

"When I was in college at UCLA, I took a playwriting course. I was all set to be a writer. But I had to take this acting class as a theater arts major. I had to do this scene in a one-act comedy. I just said this line, and then … this laugh happened. I thought, 'Whoa. This is a really good feeling. What have I been missing?'"
~ Carol Burnett ~

"I really always felt that I was going to be an actress. I had a lot of confidence in the fact that I would do well from a very early age. I didn't know how tough the business is."
~ Susan Lucci ~

"I spent a lot of my early career in the theatre—and by that I mean as an usher."
~ Edward Norton ~

"I think everything I do is my early work. I can't wait to get on to the later stuff."
~ Joseph Fiennes ~

"My mother was against me being an actress—until I introduced her to Frank Sinatra."
~ Angie Dickinson ~

"I was born Maurice Joseph Micklewhite. Imagine signing that autograph! You'd get a broken arm. So I changed my name to Michael Caine after Humphrey Bogart's The Caine Mutiny, which was playing in the theater across from the telephone booth where I learned that I'd gotten my first TV job."
~ Michael Caine ~

Ego, Pride, and Humility

"If you're smart, you'll always be humble. You can learn all you want, but there'll always be somebody who's never read a book who'll know twice what you know."
~ David Duchovny ~

"Actors are fifty percent ego, fifty percent insecure."
~ Uzo Aduba ~

"One of the easiest ways of controlling the ego is not giving it the things that it craves."
~ Stuart Wilde ~

"It is well to remember that the entire universe, with one trifling exception, is composed of others."
~ John Andrew Holmes ~

"In the light of our egos, we are all dethroned monarchs"
~ Charlie Chaplin ~

"The second show I did on TV, I was the lead. I made nine hundred dollars and I was having fun saying some other guy's words. This is a dangerous profession for the ego."
~ Telly Savalas ~

"Pride is a master of deception: when you think you're occupied in the weightiest business, that's when he has you in his spell."
~ Marcus Aurelius ~

"If you're not humble, life will visit humbleness upon you."
~ Mike Tyson ~

"If you let your head get too big, it'll break your neck."
~ Elvis Presley ~

"Ego is the anesthetic that deadens the pain of stupidity."
~ Rick Rigsby ~

"Ego is the unhealthy belief in your own importance."
~ Ryan Holiday ~

"I so despise a man who blows his own horn,
that I go to the other extreme."
~ James A. Garfield ~

"Humility is not thinking less of yourself; it is thinking of yourself less. Humility is thinking more of others. Humble people are so focused on serving others, they don't think of themselves."
~ Rick Warrren ~

"If you get your ego in your way, you will only look to other people and circumstances to blame."
~ Jocko Willink ~

"When a man realizes his littleness, his greatness can appear."
~ H.G. Wells ~

"I have an ego that's no higher than the tail of a snail."
~ Al Lewis ~

Enthusiasm

"Approach every film with the same enthusiasm, regardless of its budget."
~ Lou Diamond Phillips ~

"The importance of enthusiastic application cannot be overestimated."
~ Martin "Farmer" Burns ~

"Passion is very important to me. If you stop enjoying things, you've got to look at it, because it can lead to all kinds of depressing scenarios."
~ Nicolas Cage ~

"Learn to show enthusiasm, even when you don't feel like it."
~ H. Jackson Brown Jr. ~

"Dogs have boundless enthusiasm but no sense of shame. I should have a dog as a life coach."
~ Moby ~

"It is better to be high-spirited, even though one makes more mistakes, than to be narrow-minded and all too prudent."
~ Vincent van Gogh ~

"Enthusiasm is the electricity of life. How do you get it? You act enthusiastic until you make it a habit."
~ Gordon Parks ~

"If you've got nothing else, passion will get you through."
~ *Henry Cavill* ~

"Always go with your passions. Never ask yourself if it's realistic or not."
~ *Deepak Chopra* ~

"Creativity is a natural extension of our enthusiasm."
~ *Earl Nightingale* ~

"The secret of genius is to carry the spirit of the child into old age, which means never losing your enthusiasm."
~ *Aldous Huxley* ~

"Fall in love with what you're going to do for a living. To be able to get out of bed and do what you love to do for the rest of the day is beyond words. I'd rather be a failure in something I love than be successful in something I hate."
~ *George Burns* ~

"If you have zest and enthusiasm, you attract zest and enthusiasm. Life does give back in kind."
~ *Norman Vincent Peale* ~

"If you have passion, there is no need for excuses because your enthusiasm will trump any negative reasoning you might come up with. Enthusiasm makes excuses a nonissue."
~ *Wayne Dyer* ~

"Nothing is so contagious as enthusiasm."
~ *Samuel Taylor Coleridge* ~

Envy, Comparison, and Competition

"Other women looked on me as a rival.
And it pained me a great deal."
~ Grace Kelly ~

"The few who do are the envy of the many who only watch."
~ Jim Rohn ~

"Success makes so many people hate you. I wish it wasn't that way. It would be wonderful to enjoy success without seeing envy in the eyes of those around you."
~ Marilyn Monroe ~

"The best revenge is massive success."
~ Frank Sinatra ~

"There's always going to be someone with
a bigger toy than yours."
~ Daniel Craig ~

"Compare yourself to who you were yesterday,
not to who someone else is today."
~ Jordan Peterson ~

"One of the hardest things for most of us to put up with
is a braggart who makes good."
~ Henny Youngman ~

"One of the great flaws that we all share is that we think everyone else is cooler, everyone else is sexier; everyone else has all the answers. That was me too."

~ Tom Hiddleston ~

"Every actor has a natural animosity toward every other actor, present or absent, living or dead."

~ Louise Brooks ~

"I had a hard time treating my field as if it's horse racing, putting actors in competition against each other. I see how the industry and the studios feel it's important, but I don't really have a feeling for being in competition. I want to feel sympathetic and close to others, not opposed to them."

~ Alan Arkin ~

"I'm a believer, however naively, that someone will place me in a project because they've seen my work, rather than me being bullish or so ambitious that I get the part by any other means."

~ Joseph Fiennes ~

"Sometimes I've been to a party where no one spoke to me for a whole evening. The men, frightened by their wives or sweeties, would give me a wide berth. And the ladies would gang up in a corner to discuss my dangerous character."

~ Marilyn Monroe ~

"The flower which is single need not envy the thorns that are numerous."

~ Rabindranath Tagore ~

Exceptionalism

"Set out to do a good job, and do that job so well that the living, the dead, or the unborn couldn't do it any better."
~ Martin Luther King Jr. ~

"Integrate what you believe in every single area of your life. Take your heart to work and ask the most and best of everybody else, too."
~ Meryl Streep ~

"Sometimes, when you overreach, you pull it off and it's a thrill."
~ Francis Ford Coppola ~

"Don't ever promise more than you can deliver, but always deliver more than you promise."
~ Lou Holtz ~

"I think it is possible for ordinary people to choose to be extraordinary."
~ Elon Musk ~

"You want to be uncommon amongst uncommon people. Period."
~ David Goggins ~

"Do something wonderful, people may imitate it."
~ Albert Schweitzer ~

"The best is the enemy of the good."
~ Voltaire ~

"Repeat the following phrase to yourself twenty times a day—literally—and it will change your life forever: 'I can do anything I set my mind to if I'm willing to pay the price for greatness.'"
~ Tom Bilyeu ~

"I refuse to be another man who lived and died and wasn't significant"
~ Sagi Kalev ~

"It wasn't enough for me just to win. I also wanted to make a difference."
~ Garry Kasparov ~

"If I'm not here to maximize my potential, then what am I on Earth for?"
~ LL Cool J ~

"If you concentrate upon your strengths, usually your weaknesses will fall away and become less dominant in your life."
~ Stuart Wilde ~

"The goal is not to change who you are, but to become more of who you are at your best."
~ Sally Hogshead ~

"Too few accomplish twice as much as too many."
~ Malcolm Forbes ~

Excesses

"The fun, joy, and humor dry up in a relationship when one of the partners is swimming in gin. To my way of thinking, it is selfishness personified to see life through the bottom of a liquor bottle."
~ Ginger Rogers ~

"An alcoholic is someone you don't like who drinks as much as you do."
~ Dylan Thomas ~

"There is a quality of selfishness that is associated with an individual when they are in the depths of addiction."
~ David Dastmalchian ~

"I was in my mid-forties. I was a bulimic, and I realized if I continue with this addiction of mine, I will not be able to continue doing my life. The older you get the more damage it does; it takes longer to recover from a binge. And it was very hard."
~ Jane Fonda ~

"No one is immune from addiction; it afflicts people of all ages, races, classes, and professions."
~ Patrick J. Kennedy ~

"Marijuana is a much bigger part of the American addiction problem than most people, teens or adults, realize."
~ John Walters ~

"Drama can be an addiction. It's so, so sneaky. Jealousy—
all of those things can really send you in a lot of
different crazy directions."
~ Christian Slater ~

"Cocaine is nothing new. It's been part of Hollywood from the
outset. It's the pressure, I think. People use it to relieve that, and
for me it was about getting numb and forgetting. I did coke so I
wouldn't have to talk to anyone. For me, it was a true sedative,
a way to pull back from the world."
~ Robin Williams ~

"It did not feel like something that was going to take over
my life and destroy it. It felt like a subtle flower instead of
a manipulative demon. That's the mystery of heroin."
~ Corey Feldman ~

"What fascinates me about addiction and obsessive behavior is
that people would choose an altered state of consciousness that's
toxic and ostensibly destroys most aspects of your normal life,
because for a brief moment you feel okay."
~ Moby ~

"Whether I or anyone else accepted the concept of alcoholism as
a disease didn't matter; what mattered was that when treated as a
disease, those who suffered from it were most likely to recover."
~ Craig Ferguson ~

"Alcoholism is a disease, but it's the only one
you can get yelled at for having."
~ Mitch Hedberg ~

Failure ... and Bouncing Back!

"Acting is really about having the courage to fail in front of people."
~ Adam Driver ~

"I don't understand a way to work other than bold-facedly running towards failure."
~ Cate Blanchett ~

"I honestly think it is better to be a failure at something you love than to be a success at something you hate."
~ George Burns ~

"When one door closes, another opens. But we often look so regretfully upon the closed door that we don't see the one that has opened for us."
~ Alexander Graham Bell ~

"Even failures can turn into something positive if you just keep going. I wrote a television pilot called *Head of the Family*. CBS didn't want it. It was considered a failure. But we reworked it. A year later, it became *The Dick Van Dyke Show*."
~ Carl Reiner ~

"I can see any failure as a chance."
~ Shinya Yamanaka ~

"Failure seldom stops you. What stops you is the fear of failure."
~ Jack Lemmon ~

"When you crash and burn, you have to pick yourself up and go on and hope to make up for it."
~ Burt Reynolds ~

"To have a comeback, you have to have a setback."
~ Mr. T ~

"I still think I'm going to be fired in the first week of every new job I take. Always. In fact, before I even start a movie I'll try to get myself fired or think of a reason I should quit. I guess it's fear of failure."
~ Michelle Pfeiffer ~

"You must fail a hundred times to succeed once. That's part of it. No one succeeds the first time. It's learning how to not get disappointed with failure, to understand failure. You only learn when you fail. You don't learn when you succeed."
~ Sylvester Stallone ~

"True victory is not about finishing first; it is about finishing regardless of how many times you fall."
~ Rebecca Eilts ~

"It is by going down into the abyss that we recover the treasures of life. Where you stumble, there lies your treasure."
~ Joseph Campbell ~

"Strength does not come from winning. Your struggles develop your strengths. When you go through hardships and decide not to surrender, that is strength."
~ Arnold Schwarzenegger ~

"The act of suffering does not make you a victim—only your point of view can do that. Even loss can enrich."
~ Kevin Sorbo ~

"If you're willing to fail interestingly, you tend to succeed interestingly."
~ Edward Albee ~

"People rise out of the ashes because they are invested in the possibility of triumph over seemingly impossible odds."
~ Robert Downey Jr. ~

"Flops are a part of life's menu, and I've never been a girl to miss out on any of the courses."
~ Rosalind Russell ~

"Failure is fantastic. Don't underestimate failure."
~ David Sedaris ~

"Our task is to rise and continue."
~ Ulysses S. Grant ~

"A champion is one who gets up when he can't"
~ Jack Dempsey ~

Faith

"Day by day, as you fill your mind with faith, there will ultimately be no room left for fear. This is the one great fact that no one should forget. Master faith and you will automatically master fear."
~ Norman Vincent Peale ~

"When you come to the end of all the light you know, and it's time to step into the darkness of the unknown, faith is knowing that one of two things shall happen: Either you will be given something solid to stand on or you will be taught to fly."
~ Edward Teller ~

"I'm a believing person. I believe in God even though I can't see Him. You can't see the air in this room, right? But take it away and you're dead. And I believe there's something for us after we die. The world isn't wasteful."
~ Lillian Gish ~

"Faith is the expectancy of good. Fear is the expectancy of evil. Well, who's doing the expecting?"
~ Mary Pickford ~

"The majority of my patients consisted not of believers but of those who had lost their faith."
~ Carl Jung ~

"I find that it's hard to fully examine one's life and
not have faith be part of the discussion."
~ J. J. Abrams ~

"I live in the faith that there is a Presence and Power greater
than I am that nurtures and supports me in ways I could not
even imagine. I know that this Presence is All Knowing and
All Power and is always right where I am."
~ Ernest Holmes ~

"Faith is taking the first step even when
you can't see the whole staircase."
~ Martin Luther King Jr. ~

"Faith is the oil the takes the friction out of living."
~ Les Brown ~

"If your knees knock, kneel on them."
~ Edward R. Murrow ~

"I have never lost my faith in God."
~ Maureen O'Hara ~

"I walk by faith, not by sight."
~ Denzel Washington ~

"The errors of faith are better than the best thoughts of unbelief."
~ Thomas Russell ~

"To plant a garden is to believe in tomorrow."
~ Audrey Hepburn ~

Fame

"Just because you've done a good performance once, doesn't mean you're always going to be good. That's why some of the greatest actors in the world have gone a little bit nuts. They're saying to themselves, "What happened? You used to love me?" It's an easy trap to fall into. You just have to realize that when you're hot, you're hot, and when you're not, you're not."
~ Leonardo DiCaprio ~

"I never had a desire to be famous. I was fat. I didn't know any fat famous actresses. You know, once a fat kid, always a fat kid. Because you always think that you just look a little bit wrong or a little bit different from everyone else. And I still sort of have that.
~ Kate Winslet ~

"People are always saying they loved me in *Titanic*."
~ Cate Blanchett ~

"A celebrity is a person who works hard all his life to become well known, then wears dark glasses to avoid being recognized."
~ Fred Allen ~

"You're famous when a crazy person imagines that he's you."
~ Henny Youngman ~

"A star on a movie set is like a time bomb. That bomb has got to be defused so people can approach it without fear."
~ Jack Nicholson ~

"I disappear from the public eye and get
rediscovered quite often."
~ Burgess Meredith ~

"There was nothing lonelier than a man with a million friends."
~ William Shatner ~

"When you become a star,
you don't change—everyone else does."
~ Kirk Douglas ~

"The more you stand in the limelight, the more scarred you will
become and the more you will love the limelight."
~ Preston Sturges ~

"There is no question you get pumped up by the recognition.
Then a self-loathing sets in when you realize you're enjoying it."
~ George C. Scott ~

"Everywhere you go, there's someone shoving a chair under
your bum, and if you take out a cigarette there are eighty-four
people jumping up to light it and tell you how wonderful you
are. And you know it's not true."
~ Richard Burton ~

"You can't get spoiled if you do your own ironing."
~ Meryl Streep ~

"Some day each of us will be famous for fifteen minutes."
~ Andy Warhol ~

"There's no difference between fame and infamy now. There's a new school of professional famous people that don't do anything. They don't create anything."
~ Ricky Gervais ~

"Sometimes you have to be hidden. Sometimes people are not supposed to recognize you."
~ Tyler Perry ~

"I'd had people say, 'You'll enjoy being famous for a week, and you'll never enjoy it again.' But I don't think I had that week. I may have been working and missed that moment."
~ Matt Damon ~

"I could have been a dental hygienist with nothing bad ever appearing in print about me, but that's not how I've chosen to lead my life. I knew that you put yourself under a microscope the more famous you become."
~ Julia Roberts ~

"Man, when I'm riding with the helmet on, I'm invisible. And people just deal with me as the guy on the bike … it gives you a chance to read 'em."
~ Brad Pitt ~

"The loneliest you will get is in the most public of arenas: You will go to a place and end up in the smallest compartment possible, because it's a distraction to everybody, and you end up not getting to enjoy it like everyone else."
~ George Clooney ~

"You should prepare when you go to a public event to be public. That's when I will sign autographs. But not when you're going about your normal business."
~ *Robert Redford* ~

"I didn't have a lot of friends. I had become isolated by fame. I longed for a family and some substantive relationships. Fame is a vapor. You can't grab hold of it."
~ *Lynda Carter* ~

"The story of my life is about back entrances, side doors, secret elevators and other ways of getting in and out of places so that people won't bother me."
~ *Greta Garbo* ~

"I didn't come to Hollywood to be the girl next door. I came to be a movie star."
~ *Jayne Mansfield* ~

"On the outside, one is a star. But in reality, one is completely alone, doubting everything. To experience this loneliness of soul is the hardest thing in the world."
~ *Brigitte Bardot* ~

"I don't think much of most of the films I made, but being a movie star was something I liked very much."
~ *Joan Bennett* ~

"Going out today to take pictures of paparazzi."
~ *Steve Martin* ~

"Just because your voice reaches halfway around the world doesn't mean you are wiser than when it reached only to the end of the bar."
~ *Edward R. Murrow* ~

"One day the people who didn't believe in you will tell everyone how they met you."
~ *Johnny Depp* ~

"The first time an autograph hunter told me, 'You are my mother's favorite actress,' I aged twenty years."
~ *Ingrid Bergman* ~

"The nicest thing is to open the newspapers and not to find yourself in them."
~ *George Harrison* ~

"I hate the idea of success robbing you of your private life."
~ *Paul McCartney* ~

"I've been … chased by paparazzi, and they run lights, and they chase you and harass you the whole time. It happens all over the world, and it has certainly gotten worse. You don't know what it's like being chased by them."
~ *Tom Cruise* ~

"With paparazzi, I'm constantly trying to see my kids' view of the situation—that if I start flipping the bird or throwing punches how frightening it would be for them."
~ *Hugh Jackman* ~

"Overnight stardom can be harmful to your mental health. Yeah. It has ruined a lot of people."
~ *Clint Eastwood* ~

"I was completely unprepared for the public spectacle my private life became, and didn't like it a bit."
~ *Harrison Ford* ~

"It's a chain of accidents. When you step into Hollywood, you wind yourself into thousands of chains of accidents. If all of the thousands happen to come out exactly right —and the chance of that figures out to be one in eight million—then you'll be a star."
~ *Clark Gable* ~

"I kinda see my current position like this: Here's your five minutes in the toy store, so you gotta do all the good movies you can before Chuck Barris rings the bell."
~ *Ben Affleck* ~

"I became famous almost before I had a craft."
~ *Farrah Fawcett* ~

"Everybody in the world knew who I was before I knew who I was."
~ *Michael J. Fox* ~

"I found out when I did *The Oprah Winfrey Show* that there was a cookie jar of me. So she gave it to me. I had no idea prior to that that it even existed."
~ *Carrie Fisher* ~

"I'm doing what I love, and then I get months and months of rest. I have a lot of money for a twenty-one-year-old. I can't stand it when actors complain."
~ Jennifer Lawrence ~

"I'm makin' a lotta dough, everyone knows who you are, and who the hell cares whether you're typecast or not? Also, there's something wrong with complaining about being typecast in something you really enjoy doing."
~ Peter Falk ~

"I walk the streets, take the train, it's real simple. Some actors create their own mythology: 'Oh, I'm so famous I can't go places, because I created this mythology that I'm so famous I can't go places.'"
~ Samuel L. Jackson ~

"The thing about the wacky fans is that they're really sweet."
~ Margot Kidder ~

"The only time I'm not Hulk Hogan is when I'm behind closed doors because as soon as I walk out the front door, and somebody says hello to me, I can't just say 'hello' like Terry. When they see me, they see the blond hair, the mustache, and the bald head, they instantly think Hulk Hogan."
~ Hulk Hogan ~

"People on television have trouble with fame because audiences think they're their mates."
~ Ian McKellen ~

Family

"How do you rebel in a family of rebels?"
~ Nicolas Cage ~

"I would live with all of my sisters if I could. We've always been very close, my sisters and me."
~ Tom Cruise ~

"My dad was an absentee dad, so it was always important to me that I was part of my daughter's life, and she deserved two parents, which is part of the rationale behind us staying married for thirty years."
~ Samuel L. Jackson ~

"Now that I'm a parent, I understand why my father was in a bad mood a lot."
~ Adam Sandler ~

"It's my privilege and honor to cook three meals a day for my family, and it's a luxury on a level that I didn't even realize, because it can be relentless for me on some days. You have pride in how you take care of your family."
~ Julia Roberts ~

"Wake up in the morning, put your hand to something useful, and take care of yourself and your family."
~ John Ratzenberger ~

"The worst thing a man can admit is, 'I'm not one hundred percent fulfilled by my family.' But it doesn't mean he doesn't love his family. I love my family, but I still want to work. I still want challenges. It took me a while to fall in love with the responsibility of family life, and it was a deep thing when I did."
~ David Duchovny ~

"I think there are two ways to depict a family. One is what it's really like, and one is what the audience would like it to be. Between you and me, I think the second one is what I would prefer."
~ Aaron Spelling ~

"I resent that there is an image of perfection that is getting thinner and thinner. I've got a lovely husband and children, and I didn't lose weight to find those things."
~ Kate Winslet ~

"It's not our job to toughen our children up to face a cruel and heartless world. It's our job to raise children who will make the world a little less cruel and heartless."
~ L.R. Knost ~

"When I was nine years old, living on the south side of Chicago, my father was a minister and my mother used to scrub floors. I had seven brothers and four sisters. I told my mama, 'One of these days, I'm going to be big and strong and buy you a beautiful house.' That's all I've ever wanted to do with my life, is to take care of my mother."
~ Mr. T ~

"My mother had lots and lots of children who didn't survive."
~ Dom DeLuise ~

"The biggest place I look for validation is from my mother. That's the little girl in me that will never grow up."
~ Naomi Watts ~

"All of my life I have asked the question, 'Who would I be if I had grown up in a loving home?' And I have no way to answer it. I don't know if I would be placid and satisfied with whatever is around me—a happy, jolly, sedentary person."
~ Ellen Burstyn ~

"I didn't know that my sister was really my mother until I was thirty-seven years old. But life has taught me that there have been a lot of things that I didn't know."
~ Jack Nicholson ~

"Dysfunctional families have sired a number of pretty good actors."
~ Gene Hackman ~

"Nobody became an actor because he had a good childhood."
~ William H. Macy ~

"There are no illegitimate children—only illegitimate parents."
~ Leon R. Yankwich ~

"Family means no one gets left behind or forgotten."
~ David Ogden Stiers ~

Fear

"To fear is one thing. To let fear grab you by the tail and swing you around is another."
~ Katherine Paterson ~

"Once you've been really bad in a movie, there's a certain kind of fearlessness you develop."
~ Jack Nicholson ~

"There is nothing in the dark that isn't there when the lights are on."
~ Rod Serling ~

"Fear kills more people than death."
~ General George Patton ~

"Desire is the perfect antidote for fear."
~ Dennis Waitley ~

"Curiosity will conquer fear even more than bravery will."
~ James Stephens ~

"I live my life through fear. If I'm afraid of it, I'll do it just so I'm not afraid of it anymore."
~ Jeremy Renner ~

"People die of fright and live of confidence."
~ Henry David Thoreau ~

"I've always felt that if you back down from a fear, the ghost of that fear never goes away. It diminishes people. So I've always said yes to the thing I'm most scared about."
~ *Hugh Jackman* ~

"Fear is possibly the greatest motivation there is. But, as I said before, by pretending not to fear, you can make it work for you and get the job done."
~ *Lee Marvin* ~

"He who fears something gives it power over him."
~ *Moorish Proverb* ~

"The only way to get rid of my fears is to make films about them."
~ *Alfred Hitchcock* ~

"Fear is an extraordinary artist, stimulating the mind to reminisce, as if to divine where fairytale meets horror novel."
~ *Kevin Sorbo* ~

"Nothing in life is to be feared, it is only to be understood. Now is the time to understand more, so that we may fear less."
~ *Marie Curie* ~

"Scared is what you're feeling. Brave is what you're doing."
~ *Emma Donoghue* ~

"Some say if only my fears and doubts will leave, then I will get to work. But instead you should get to work, then your fears and doubts will leave."
~ *D.L. Moody* ~

"I learned that courage was not the absence of fear, but the triumph over it. The brave man is not he who does not feel afraid, but he who conquers that fear."
~ Nelson Mandela ~

"Fear is evidence of ignorance."
~ Myles Munroe ~

"What we fear doing most is usually what we most need to do."
~ Timothy Ferriss ~

"Be specific. Fear is a generality. Be specific."
~ Michael Shurtleff ~

"Keep your fears to yourself, but share your courage."
~ Robert Louis Stevenson ~

"Face a situation fearlessly, and there is no situation to face; it falls away of its own weight."
~ Florence Scovel Shinn ~

"Feel the fear and do it anyway."
~ Susan Jeffers ~

"Great work is done by people who are not afraid to be great."
~ Fernando Flores ~

"They will take a role that scares them over a role that doesn't. That's another thing I like about actors."
~ James Lipton ~

Feelings and Emotions

"Out of your vulnerabilities will come your strength."
~ Sigmund Freud ~

"I am a person who is trained to look other people in the eye. But I can't look into the eyes of everyone who wants to look into mine. I can't emotionally cope with that kind of volume. Sunglasses are part of my armor."
~ Jack Nicholson ~

"I put on an act sometimes, and people think I'm insensitive. Really, it's like a kind of armor because I'm too sensitive. If there are two hundred people in a room and one of them doesn't like me, I've got to get out."
~ Marlon Brando ~

"If one person in a thousand criticized me while all the others cheered, I didn't hear the cheers."
~ Dorothy Dandridge ~

"A person can destroy me with two words. It can just be the way they say them, the inflection."
~ Peter Sellers ~

"My defenses were so great. The cocky rock and roll hero who knows all the answers was actually a terrified guy who didn't know how to cry. Simple."
~ John Lennon ~

"Feelings are not facts."
~ GiGi Erneta ~

"Remind yourself that you have the power to choose how you feel."
~ Mike Cernovich ~

"We often add to our pain and suffering by being overly sensitive, over-reacting to minor things, and sometimes taking things too personally."
~ Dalai Lama ~

"Emotional self-control is the result of hard work, not an inherent skill."
~ Travis Bradberry ~

"The night I won the Emmy, I probably cried for three hours on and off."
~ Brad Garrett ~

"Follow your heart, but take your brain with you."
~ Alfred Adler ~

"Mental pain is less dramatic than physical pain, but it is more common and also more hard to bear. The frequent attempt to conceal mental pain increases the burden: it is easier to say "My tooth is aching" than to say "My heart is broken.""
~ C. S. Lewis ~

"I weep at everything."
~ Chris Evans ~

Focus

"Always remember, your focus determines your reality."
~ *George Lucas* ~

"You're always carrying something that's interfering. It's like static noise that doesn't have to be there, and you have to school yourself to clean that out."
~ *Bill Pullman* ~

"It is your work to clear away the mass of encumbering material of thoughts, so that you may bring into plain view the precious thing at the center of the mass."
~ *Robert Collier* ~

"Focus on where you want to go, not on what you fear."
~ *Anthony Robbins* ~

"The main thing is to keep the main thing the main thing."
~ *Stephen Covey* ~

"Pay attention to the vital few. Ignore the trivial many."
~ *Jon Paul DeJoria* ~

"Don't get caught up in the things that don't matter."
~ *Tilman Fertitta* ~

"Take control and choose to focus on what is important in your life. Those who cannot live fully often become destroyers of life."
~ *Anaïs Nin* ~

"The ability to be fully present makes you stand out from the crowd; it makes you memorable. When you're fully present, even a five-minute conversation can create a "wow" effect, as well as an emotional connection."
~ Olivia Fox Cabane ~

"I learned many things working with Cary Grant. He has such tremendous concentration. Many actors do not have the courage to stand still. Cary Grant knows how to concentrate, how to look directly at you, but always with great relaxation."
~ Sophia Loren ~

"Never be so focused on what you're looking for that you overlook the thing you actually find."
~ Ann Patchett ~

We can always choose to perceive things differently. We can focus on what's wrong in our life, or we can focus on what's right."
~ Marianne Williamson ~

"I learned long ago to focus on things you can control and don't even pay attention to things you don't"
~ Bryan Cranston ~

"It's never too late. Don't focus on what was taken away. Find something to replace it, and acknowledge the blessing you have."
~ Drew Barrymore ~

"Focus like a laser, not a flashlight."
~ Michael Jordan ~

Getting Started

"Before discovering theater, I was sloughing off and didn't have any passion for school. Then I couldn't get enough. All of a sudden, I was getting good parts in all of these plays. I just loved it. I started getting A's in acting, directing, and technical theater. I found something that clicked."
~ Gary Sinise ~

"I never planned on being an actress, just as I never planned on being a model. I went to law and international relations school. It wasn't my direction. It kind of happened to me. And because it wasn't my dream when I started, I wasn't star-struck."
~ Gal Gadot ~

"My parents wanted me to be a lawyer. But I don't think I would have been very happy. I'd be in front of the jury singing."
~ Jennifer Lopez ~

"I hitched to London on a lorry, looking for adventure. I was dropped at Euston Station and was trying to find a hostel. I passed the Royal Academy of Dramatic Art, and walked in just to case the joint."
~ Peter O'Toole ~

"I decided to take a stab at acting. I entered the American Academy of Dramatic Art, where one teacher told me I'd never make it—I was too tall."
~ Fred Gwynne ~

"I was discouraged at drama school,
along with most of my peers."
~ Sigourney Weaver ~

"You start where you can get an opportunity, you take everything that you can do to gain entrance. You do the little work and you try to find people who can teach you."
~ Jon Voight ~

"I went in the Marines when I was sixteen. I spent four and a half years in the Marines and then came right to New York to be an actor. And then seven years later, I got my first job."
~ Gene Hackman ~

"I left Scotland when I was sixteen because I had no qualifications for anything but the Navy, having left school at thirteen."
~ Sean Connery ~

"I came back from the war and ugly heroes were in."
~ Robert Mitchum ~

"I became an actor because I believed I was a failure. In acting, because so few of us ever get work, I could feel proud and fail with dignity."
~ Dustin Hoffman ~

"When I graduated from Santa Monica High in 1927, I was voted the girl most likely to succeed. I didn't realize it would take so long."
~ Gloria Stuart ~

Goals

"Setting goals is the first step in turning
the invisible into the visible."
~ Anthony Robbins ~

"Our dreams and goals are never completely realized.
They are always there before our eyes, but always just
slightly out of reach. And so, as we strive to fulfill our vision,
we must make the most of every living moment."
~ *Jacqueline Kennedy Onassis* ~

"Enjoy where you are on the way to where you're going."
~ *Joel Osteen* ~

"Goals are dreams we convert to plans and take action to fulfill."
~ *Zig Ziglar* ~

"If you set your goals ridiculously high and it's a failure,
you will fail above everyone else's success."
~ *James Cameron* ~

"Set a goal so big that in the process of achieving it
you become someone worth being."
~ *Jim Rohn* ~

"Goals are dreams with deadlines."
~ *Diana Scharf* ~

"There is no finish line.
When you reach one goal, find a new one."
~ *Chuck Norris* ~

"My interest in life comes from setting myself huge, apparently unachievable challenges, and trying to rise above them."
~ *Richard Branson* ~

"Give yourself an even greater challenge than the one you are trying to master and you will develop the powers necessary to overcome the original difficulty."
~ *William J. Bennett* ~

"Real results come from putting your momentary needs on hold to pursue larger, more important goals."
~ *Travis Bradberry* ~

"If you have attention on your problems, your goals aren't big enough."
~ *Grant Cardone* ~

"Here's to getting unstuck and moving forward."
~ *Barry Moltz* ~

"Get yourself a goal worth working for."
~ *Dr. Maxwell Maltz* ~

"While goals disappear the moment you achieve them, the journey never disappears."
~ *Mike Hernacki* ~

Happiness

"Everyday happiness means getting up in the morning, and you can't wait to finish your breakfast. You can't wait to do your exercises. You can't wait to put on your clothes. You can't wait to get out—and you can't wait to come home, because the soup is hot."
~ George Burns ~

"You have to be willing to get happy about nothing."
~ Andy Warhol ~

"Happiness is nothing but everyday living seen through a veil."
~ Zora Neale Hurston ~

"We can all be agents in the conspiracy to make this world a happier place."
~ Daniel Goleman ~

"I really do believe I can accomplish a great deal with a big grin, I know some people find that disconcerting, but that doesn't matter."
~ Beverly Sills ~

"Ever since happiness heard your name, it has been running through the streets trying to find you."
~ Hafiz ~

"If you are not happy, act the happy man. Happiness will come later. So also with faith. If you are in despair, act as though you believe. Faith will come afterwards."
~ Isaac Bashevis Singer ~

"Even if you're unhappy, just pretend that you're happy. Eventually, your smile will be contagious to yourself. I had to learn that, I used to think, 'I'm being fake,' but you know what? Better to be fake and happy than real and miserable."
~ Evangeline Lilly ~

"The noblest art is that of making others happy."
~ P.T. Barnum ~

"The only way on Earth to multiply happiness is to divide it."
~ Paul Scherer ~

"Happiness is a moving target."
~ Kinky Friedman ~

"Happiness is a way station between too little and too much."
~ Channing Pollock ~

"To be without some of the things you want is an indispensable part of happiness."
~ Bertrand Russell ~

"Human happiness and moral duty are inseparably connected."
~ George Washington ~

"Don't waste a minute not being happy. If one window closes, run to the next window—or break down a door."
~ *Brooke Shields* ~

"I'm happy to report that our capacity for happiness is the same as it has always been. Being happy is an inside job."
~ *Dr. Richard Carlson* ~

"It's difficult for people sometimes to recognize when they're happy. People sometimes seem to me to be afraid to be happy."
~ *Jack Nicholson* ~

"It takes courage to be happy."
~ *Mark Van Doren* ~

"True happiness is not contained in what you get. Happiness is contained in what you become."
~ *Jim Rohn* ~

"If you are not happy, you had better stop worrying about it and see what treasures you can pluck from your own brand of unhappiness."
~ *Robertson Davies* ~

"Happiness often sneaks in through a door you didn't know you left open."
~ *John Barrymore* ~

"When happiness shows up, give it a comfortable seat."
~ *Milton Berle* ~

"If you want to be happy, be."
~ Leo Tolstoy ~

"The search for happiness is one of the chief sources of unhappiness."
~ Eric Hoffer ~

"We either make ourselves happy or miserable. The amount of work is the same."
~ Carlos Castaneda ~

"We do not sing because we are happy. We are happy because we sing."
~ William James ~

"The happiest people are the people with the best attitudes, not the best lives."
~ Bob Lonsberry ~

"Let us go singing as far as we go; the road will be much less tedious."
~ Virgil ~

"If you observe a really happy man, you will find him building a boat, writing a symphony, educating his son, growing double dahlias in his garden. He will not be searching for happiness as if it were a collar button that has rolled under the radiator."
~ W. Beran Wolfe ~

"If you see someone without a smile, give him yours."
~ June Allyson ~

Hard Work

"I will not be out-worked. Period."
~ Will Smith ~

"Be humble. Be hungry. And always be
the hardest worker in the room."
~ Dwayne Johnson ~

"The person who wants to make it has to sweat. There are no
short cuts. And you've got to have the guts to be hated."
~ Bette Davis ~

"I had no natural gift to be anything—not an athlete, not an
actor, not a writer, not a director, a painter of garden porches—
not anything. So I've worked really hard, because
nothing ever came easily to me."
~ Paul Newman ~

"I was not a born actress. No one knows it better than I. If I had
any latent talent, I have had to work hard, listen carefully, do
things over and over and then over again in order to bring it out."
~ Jean Harlow ~

"I believed in the concept of over-performing. I believe anyone
can achieve their goals in life if they over-perform, and that
means you have to work ten times harder than anybody you see."
~ Stephen J. Cannell ~

"I'm impressed with the people from Chicago.
Hollywood is hype, New York is talk, Chicago is work."
~ Michael Douglas ~

"Hard work without talent is a frustration, but
talent without hard work is a tragedy."
~ Robert Half ~

"There are no secrets to success. It is the result of preparation,
hard work, and learning from failure."
~ General Colin Powell ~

"The heights by great men reached and kept were not attained
by sudden flight. But they, while their companions slept,
were toiling upward in the night."
~ Henry Wadsworth Longfellow ~

"Men talk of victory as of something fortunate. Work is victory.
Wherever work is done victory is obtained."
~ Ralph Waldo Emerson ~

"I always wanted to do my best. I got nothing free.
I had to work hard."
~ Greta Garbo ~

"If I have one advantage, it's that I will try
to work harder than the next guy."
~ Jay Leno ~

"The bridge between reality and a dream is work."
~ Jared Leto ~

"I don't go to bed. I pass out."
~ David Meltzer ~

"Nothing will work unless you do."
~ Maya Angelou ~

"If you rest, you rust."
~ Helen Hayes ~

"Work is more fun than fun."
~ Noel Coward ~

"The hardest work of all? Doing nothing."
~ Malcolm Forbes ~

"The test of a vocation is the love of the drudgery it involves."
~ Logan Pearsall Smith ~

'I never work hard when I am working;
I only work hard when I am not working."
~ Irving Caesar ~

"In a professional once engaged, the performance of the job comes first."
~ Garson Kanin ~

"You can't wait for inspiration.
You have to go after it with a club."
~ Jack London ~

Health and Fitness

"A couple of years ago, before I had to start working out for X-Men, my diet was horrendous. Now I pretty much eat healthily just because I don't really have a tolerance for unhealthy food anymore—I feel so really groggy after I eat it. I'm into eating healthily and eating the right proportions, working out whenever I can."
~ Sophie Turner ~

"Laughing is the best calorie burner."
~ Audrey Hepburn ~

"I do isometrics in church so while I'm doing my soul some good, I'm doing my body some good, too."
~ Grace Kelly ~

"An actor is supposed to be a sensitive instrument. Isaac Stern takes good care of his violin. What if everybody jumped on his violin?"
~ Marilyn Monroe ~

"What musical performers bring to straight characterizations is that physical flexibility that comes with knowing your body so well. A lot of actors are terribly awkward. Terribly. And I think it's so important for them, when they're young, to work on their physical selves."
~ Rita Moreno ~

"The *All My Children* studio was near Lincoln Center,
and I used to see all the ballerinas and the dancers,
and I thought, I don't want to bulk up; I want to have long,
lean, toned muscles. And I found out that through Pilates,
you can achieve those strong, lean dancer muscles."
~ *Susan Lucci* ~

"I'm not overweight, I'm just nine inches too short."
~ *Shelly Winters* ~

"I am going on a diet for the next hour."
~ *Steve Martin* ~

"If it came in a bottle, everybody would have a good body."
~ *Cher* ~

"Most of the people I know who work out seriously do so
because they have such an amazing outlook on life.
To be who I want to be, I'm going to work out to
be more positive, more active. It's proactive."
~ *John Krasinski* ~

"Sickness comes on horseback and departs on foot."
~ *Dutch Proverb* ~

"I smoked three packs a day.
There was hardly time to do anything else."
~ *Mary Tyler Moore* ~

"Now that I'm gone, I tell you, don't smoke."
~ *Yul Brynner* ~

A Higher Power

"My films must let every man, woman, and child know that God loves them, that I love them, and that peace and salvation will become a reality only when they all learn to love each other."
~ Frank Capra ~

"Perhaps they are not stars in the sky, but rather openings where our loved ones shine down to let us know they are happy."
~ Native Alaskan Proverb ~

"How could you have had such a wonderful life as me if there wasn't a God directing?"
~ Maureen O'Hara ~

"Life is full of miracles, but they're not always the ones we pray for."
~ Eve Arden ~

"If you see what needs to be repaired and how to repair it, then you have found a piece of the world that God has left for you to complete. But if you only see what is wrong and what is ugly in the world, then it is you yourself that needs repair."
~ Menachem Mendel Schneerson ~

"People are like stained glass windows. They sparkle and shine when the sun's out, but when the darkness sets in, their true beauty is revealed only if there is light within."
~ Elizabeth Kubler-Ross ~

"When the road looks rough ahead, remember the 'Man Upstairs' and the word 'Hope.' Hang onto both and tough it out."
~ John Wayne ~

"Never place a period where God has placed a comma."
~ Gracie Allen ~

"When the stars are twinkling, an angel awaits your prayers."
~ Kathryn Schein ~

"I believe that there is God in all of us."
~ Michael Landon ~

"By learning to contact, listen to, and act on our intuition, we can directly connect to the higher power of the universe and allow it to become our guiding force."
~ Shakti Gawain ~

"All inspiration comes from a higher power. The body is a shell. The creative spot is from God. You hear voices, everybody does. When you get older, you refer to it as intuition."
~ Eddie Murphy ~

"I've always believed in a higher power. You can call it God, you can call it Jesus, Krishna, Buddha, Allah, I don't care. I really believe we are all a part of God."
~ Olivia Hussey ~

"I just want to believe in a higher power. That's a good way to live."
~ Eva Longoria ~

Hooray for Hollywood!

"I'd move to Los Angeles if Australia and New Zealand were swallowed up by a huge tidal wave, if there was a bubonic plague in England, and if the continent of Africa disappeared from some Martian attack."
~ Russell Crowe ~

"L.A.'s a very hard place to be unless you have people there that love you. It can be very, very lonely, and it can eat you up if you don't take care of yourself. In L.A., nobody wants to talk to each other, everybody's giving each other catty looks."
~ Scarlett Johansson ~

"You can't find true affection in Hollywood because everyone does the fake affection so well."
~ Carrie Fisher ~

"It's said in Hollywood that you should always forgive your enemies—because you never know when you'll have to work with them."
~ Lana Turner ~

"Hollywood is a goofy place. But I like it. It's the perfect mummers' home. If one weren't a little mad, one wouldn't be there."
~ Charles Laughton ~

"Hollywood must have been terrific once."
~ Peter Finch ~

"I hated Hollywood. It's a town without pity. Only success counts. I know of no other place in the world where so many people suffer from nervous breakdowns, where there are so many alcoholics, neurotics and so much unhappiness."
~ Grace Kelly ~

"I'll miss Hollywood. Of the twenty friends I thought I had, I'll miss the six I really had."
~ Lauren Bacall ~

"Hollywood is like an empty wastebasket."
~ Ginger Rogers ~

"Hollywood is a place where they'll pay you a thousand dollars for a kiss and fifty cents for your soul."
~ Marilyn Monroe ~

"Hollywood has to, at some point, admit that what they produce does affect the minds of people … If you just want to shock 'em … society will pay the price for that at some point."
~ John Ratzenberger ~

"Hollywood is the Sodom and Gomorrah of today. It's a world I avoid because it's destroying our culture."
~ Evangeline Lilly ~

"Lionel Barrymore first played my grandfather, later my father, and finally, he played my husband. If he'd lived, I'm sure I would have played his mother. That's the way it is in Hollywood. The men get younger and the women get older."
~ Lillian Gish ~

"In Europe, an actor is an artist. In Hollywood,
if he isn't working, he's a bum."
~ Anthony Quinn ~

"I sure lost my musical direction in Hollywood.
My songs were the same conveyer belt mass production,
just like most of my movies were."
~ Elvis Presley ~

"What's fascinating is, people in Washington would rather
spend time in Hollywood, and people in Hollywood
would rather spend time in Washington."
~ Arnold Schwarzenegger ~

"My life in Montana is so diverse from my Hollywood life
that it even feels odd for me to go from one life to the other."
~ Andie MacDowell ~

"Hollywood is what you make it; you have to choose company
with care because you become what they are."
~ Bonnie Hunt ~

"You can't judge Hollywood by superficial impressions.
After you get past the artificial tinsel
you get down to the real tinsel."
~ Samuel Goldwyn ~

"Hollywood was a lot like a Charles Dickens novel. It could be
the best of places; it could be the worst of places."
~ Brad Thor ~

Humor

"Humor is a social lubricant that helps us get over some of the bad spots."
~ Steve Allen ~

"I like to see people laugh who are normally serious."
~ Jimmy Fallon ~

"If we couldn't laugh, we would all go insane."
~ Jimmy Buffett ~

"Humor is just another defense against the universe."
~ Mel Brooks ~

"You can't make up anything anymore. The world itself is a satire. All you're doing is recording it."
~ Art Buchwald ~

"To truly laugh, you must be able to take your pain, and play with it."
~ Charlie Chaplin ~

"Laugh at yourself first, before anyone else can."
~ Elsa Maxwell ~

"You grow up the day you have your first real laugh at yourself."
~ Ethel Barrymore ~

"Live by this credo: have a little laugh at life and look around you for happiness instead of sadness. Laughter has always brought me out of unhappy situations."
~ *Red Skelton* ~

"It is difficult for people to appreciate their own laughter unless you show them some pathos along the way."
~ *Jackie Gleason* ~

"Laughter is an instant vacation."
~ *Milton Berle* ~

"People of humor are always in some degree people of genius."
~ *Samuel Taylor Coleridge* ~

"I try not to worry about what that's going to look like. If you worry about looking stupid, that's when you look really stupid."
~ *Rob Schneider* ~

"The most terrible fear that anybody should have is not war, is not a disease, not cancer or heart problems or food poisoning— it's a man or a woman without a sense of humor."
~ *Jonathan Winters* ~

"Mr. Magoo's appeal lies in our hostility toward an older generation. But he's not only nearsighted physically; his mind is selective of what it sees, too. That is where the humor, the satire lies, in the difference between what he thinks he sees and reality as we see it."
~ *Jim Backus* ~

"I can't do comedy that is cutting and vicious. If I knew I'd said something that was going to make someone feel bad, well, that supersedes everything."
~ Eugene Levy ~

"I learned to have a sense of humor. As an undiagnosed dyslexic, you spend a third of your time trying to figure out what's wrong with you, a third of your time trying to figure out why you can't figure it out and the final third trying to cover up the shame and humiliation."
~ Henry Winkler ~

"What soap is to the body, laughter is to the soul. Laughter is the shortest distance between two people."
~ Victor Borge ~

"I have seen what a laugh can do. It can transform almost unbearable tears into something bearable, even hopeful."
~ Bob Hope ~

"I love people who make me laugh. I honestly think it's the thing I like most, to laugh. It cures a multitude of ills. It's probably the most important thing in a person."
~ Audrey Hepburn ~

"A sense of humor is just common sense dancing."
~ William James ~

"I think of Mike Myers as the Buster Keaton of today. I think he's brought us something so special."
~ Robert Wagner ~

Iconic Roles

"I'm thrilled that *Wonder Woman* and that character endures because every actor wants a role that has some positive affect and causes people to smile or have good memories and to endure. It doesn't just go away, fade away. It's been twenty-five years that it's been off the air and so it still surprises me when younger people recognize me or know my work."
~ Lynda Carter ~

"I meet young women who say Batgirl was their role model. They say it's because it was the first time they ever felt girls could do the same thing guys could do, and sometimes better. I think that's lovely."
~ Yvonne Craig ~

"I'd gotten to know quite a few mafioso, and all of them told me they loved the picture because I had played the Godfather with dignity. Even today, I can't pay a check in Little Italy."
~ Marlon Brando ~

"It's amazing to find that so many people, who I thought really knew me, could have thought that *Sunset Blvd.* was autobiographical. I've got nobody floating in my swimming pool."
~ Gloria Swanson ~

"For some people, I will be Forrest Gump for the rest of my life. But that's okay. That's a good thing."
~ Tom Hanks ~

"It's a wonderful thing to be able to make fun of yourself and to do it in a way that sort of preserves your dignity but, at the same time, lets you play the theater of the absurd."
~ Adam West ~

"Had I not done Shakespeare, Pinter, Moliere and things such as *Godspell*—I played Judas in a hugely successful production before I did *Elm Street*—I'd probably be on a psychiatrist's couch saying: 'Freddy ruined me.' But I'd already done thirteen movies and years of non-stop theatre."
~ Robert Englund ~

"I never saw *Titanic* as a springboard for bigger films or bigger pay checks. I knew it could have been that, but I knew it would have destroyed me."
~ Kate Winslet ~

"I have always hated that damn James Bond. I'd like to kill him."
~ Sean Connery ~

"I'm the worst Bond, according to the Internet. Generally hated!"
~ Roger Moore ~

"God, as a child, I was so embarrassed when the kids would call me 'Olive Oyl,' because it meant you were skinny as a rail, you had sparrow legs, and an Adam's apple. I mean, who wants to admit she was born to play Olive Oyl?"
~ Shelley Duvall ~

"I can never get rid of *The Rifleman,* and I don't want to. It's a good image."
~ *Chuck Connors* ~

"I must say, 'The Skipper' has become my alter ego. I'm one and the same now."
~ *Alan Hale Jr.* ~

"*Gunsmoke, Wagon Train, The Dakotas*—you name a Western, I did it. I was always the bad guy in Westerns. I played more bad guys than you can shake a stick at until I played the Professor. Then I couldn't get a job being a bad guy."
~ *Russell Johnson* ~

"People thank me for giving them a break from life."
~ *Bob Denver* ~

"I made sixty movies before *Kojak* with some of the biggest names in the business, and people would still say, 'There goes what's-his-name.'"
~ *Telly Savalas* ~

"Every actor's greatest ambition is to create his own, definite and original role, a character with which he will always be identified. In my case, that role was Dracula."
~ *Bela Lugosi* ~

"The monster was the best friend I ever had."
~ *Boris Karloff* ~

"I don't play monsters. I play men besieged by fate and out for revenge."
~ ***Vincent Price*** ~

"When Rosalind Hicks, Agatha Christie's daughter, first saw me, she said, 'That's not Poirot.' I said, 'It is now, my dear.'"
~ ***Peter Ustinov*** ~

"I would embrace the character, because it won't do any good if you don't. And another thing: Don't whine or talk trash about it. I don't think you ever demean to your public what you've done. You're insulting them if you demean your work."
~ ***Barbara Eden*** ~

"I have a feeling when I'm eighty years old I'm going to get a phone call: 'There's going to be another *Rocky*.'"
~ ***Talia Shire*** ~

"Everyone has his own little Hulk inside him."
~ ***Lou Ferrigno*** ~

"As a kid, you run around the house pretending to be a superhero, and now to be doing it as a job, I feel very lucky."
~ ***Chris Hemsworth*** ~

"The thing about playing gods, whether you're playing Thor and Loki or Greco Roman gods or Indian gods or characters in any mythology, the reason that gods were invented was because they were basically larger versions of ourselves."
~ ***Tom Hiddleston*** ~

Imagination

"Imagination is more important than knowledge."
~Albert Einstein ~

"True imagination is not fanciful daydreaming;
it is fire from heaven."
~ Ernest Holmes ~

"Operate out of your imagination, not your memory."
~ Les Brown ~

"Stop the habit of wishful thinking and start the habit
of thoughtful wishes."
~ Mary Martin ~

"I was pretty ambitious. I felt like I had a good imagination
and vision for my life. And I had people telling me, 'You are
driving the vehicle of your life here. You are the master
of your own destiny in a sense. Do whatever you want to do.'"
~ Tobey Maguire ~

"Thus, man of all creatures is more than a creature, he is also
a creator. Man alone can direct his success mechanism
by the use of imagination, or imaging ability."
~ Dr. Maxwell Maltz ~

"Imagination means nothing without doing."
~ Charlie Chaplin ~

"Never limit yourself because of others' limited imagination; never limit others because of your own limited imagination."
~ Mae Jemison ~

"The imagination is closer to the actor than real life— more agreeable, more comfortable."
~ Stella Adler ~

"Movies are the art form most like man's imagination."
~ Francis Ford Coppola ~

"Everything you can imagine is real"
~ Pablo Picasso ~

"The best use of imagination is creativity. The worst use of imagination is anxiety."
~ Deepak Chopra ~

"The world of reality has its limits; the world of imagination is boundless."
~ Jean-Jacques Rousseau ~

"Imagination is the golden-eyed monster that never sleeps. It must be fed; it cannot be ignored."
~ Patricia A. McKillip ~

"Reality can be beaten with enough imagination."
~ Mark Twain ~

"You can't do it unless you can imagine it."
~ George Lucas ~

Individuality

"In order to be irreplaceable one must always be different."
~ *Coco Chanel* ~

"All creative intellectual work consists of the development of individuality. The very essence of motion picture making is to encourage originality. To bring out individual characteristics. The famous stars of the stage, film and literature have been great because, at some point, they differed from everyone else. They had a flavor all their own."
~ *Mack Sennett* ~

"I always wanted to be somebody, but now I realize I should have been more specific."
~ *Lily Tomlin* ~

"If you ask me to play myself, I will not know what to do. I do not know who or what I am."
~ *Peter Sellers* ~

"I don't know who the hell Paul Lynde is or why he's funny, and I prefer it to be a mystery to me. An actor shouldn't undergo psychoanalysis, because there are a lot of things you're better off not knowing."
~ *Paul Lynde* ~

"I was the kid next door's imaginary friend."
~ *Emo Philips* ~

"People who fit do not seek.
The seekers are people who do not fit."
~ T.D. Jakes ~

"I am not strange. I am just not normal."
~ Salvador Dali ~

"You have to give people the pleasure of giving you."
~ Rob Reiner ~

"I will not be a common man. I will stir the smooth sands of monotony."
~ Peter O'Toole ~

"No one ever made a difference by being like everyone else."
~ P.T. Barnum ~

"Being like everybody is the same as being nobody."
~ Rod Serling ~

"Always be a first-rate version of yourself, instead of a second-rate version of somebody else."
~ Judy Garland ~

"If I can't be me, I don't want to be anybody. I was born that way."
~ Joan Crawford ~

"I became an actor so I didn't have to be myself."
~ Mark Ruffalo ~

"I pretended to be somebody I wanted to be until finally I became that person. Or he became me."
~ *Cary Grant* ~

"Gregory Peck is the hottest thing in town. Some say he is a second Gary Cooper. Actually, he is the first Gregory Peck."
~ *Gregory Peck* ~

"Sometimes I wonder if I'm doing a Jimmy Stewart imitation myself."
~ *James Stewart* ~

"All that anyone needs to imitate me is two soft-boiled eggs and a bedroom voice."
~ *Peter Lorre* ~

"You are a one-time mega event in the universe. No other person has, or ever will have, the unique blend of talents, strengths, perspective, and gifts that you have."
~ *Marie Forleo* ~

"You have to remember the value of your individuality—that you have something special and different to offer that nobody else can."
~ *Jennifer Lopez* ~

"But to do this kind of work, you have to be very strong, otherwise you lose your personality, your identity. You don't know who you are. It's fantastic because I've been living thousands of lives, not only my life."
~ *Claudia Cardinale* ~

"I passionately hate the idea of being with it. I think an artist has always to be out of step with his time."
~ *Orson Welles* ~

"I don't play roles everybody likes. I'd rather have a career I'm proud of. Like everyone else, I need to eat. But I'm a very un-businesslike person, and I keep my price low. I'm not a mass product. I'm not everyone's cup of tea."
~ *Amanda Plummer* ~

"Unless you are unique, your opinion goes out the window."
~ *Dianne Wiest* ~

"Normal is not something to aspire to, it's something to get away from."
~ *Jodie Foster* ~

"Normal gets you nowhere."
~ *Kelly Cutrone* ~

"The things you get fired over when you're young are the very same things you get lifetime achievement awards for when you're old."
~ *Francis Ford Coppola* ~

"If you do things differently, success will follow you like a shadow, and you can't get rid of it."
~ *Sheldon Adelson* ~

"If you want to be an anomaly, you've got to act like one."
~ *Gary Vaynerchuk* ~

"Be an individualist—and an individual. You'll be amazed at how much faster you get ahead."
~ J. Paul Getty ~

"I invented myself."
~ Jerry Della Femina ~

"Everybody is identical in their secret unspoken belief that way deep down they are different from everyone else."
~ David Foster Wallace ~

"There is no me. I do not exist. There used to be a me but I had it surgically removed."
~ Peter Sellers ~

"You have to be odd to be number one."
~ Theodore Seuss Geisel ~

"Whoso would be a man must be a nonconformist."
~ Ralph Waldo Emerson ~

"In yourself right now is all the place you've got."
~ Flannery O'Connor ~

"Resistance to the organized mass can be affected only by the man who is as well organized in his individuality as the mass itself."
~ Carl Jung ~

"Wanted: a man who will not lose his individuality in a crowd, a man who has the courage of his convictions, who is not afraid to say 'No,' though all the world say 'Yes.'"
~ Orison Swett Marden ~

Life

"Mellow doesn't always make for a good story,
but it makes for a good life."
~ Anne Hathaway ~

"Life, like poker, has an element of risk. It shouldn't be avoided.
It should be faced."
~ Edward Norton ~

"Life is unfair, but remember it is unfair in your favor."
~ Peter Ustinov ~

"Life is what we make it. Always has been, always will be."
~ Grandma Moses ~

"Life is short, even for those who live a long time,
and we must live for the few who know and appreciate us,
who judge and absolve us, and for whom we have
the same affection and indulgence."
~ Sarah Bernhardt ~

"Life is full of strange absurdities, which, strangely enough,
do not even need to appear plausible, since they are true."
~ Luigi Pirandello ~

"Life is a tragedy when seen in close-up,
but a comedy in long shot."
~ Charlie Chaplin ~

"The difference between school and life? In school, you're taught a lesson and then given a test. In life, you're given a test that teaches you a lesson."
~ *Tom Bodett* ~

"Life's like a play: it's not the length, but the excellence of the acting that matters."
~ *Seneca* ~

"Life is the original do-it-yourself project."
~ *Henny Youngman* ~

"A life is not important except in the impact it has on other lives."
~ *Jackie Robinson* ~

"Life is hard. After all, it kills you."
~ *Katharine Hepburn* ~

"We are all born to die—the difference is the intensity with which we choose to live."
~ *Gina Lollobrigida* ~

"The big question is whether you are going to be able to say a hearty yes to your adventure."
~ *Joseph Campbell* ~

"Life is either a daring adventure or nothing."
~ *Helen Keller* ~

"Life would be so wonderful if we only knew what to do with it."
~ *Greta Garbo* ~

Love

"Love is an act of endless forgiveness, a tender look which becomes a habit."
~ Peter Ustinov ~

"Don't waste your love on somebody who doesn't value it."
~ William Shakespeare ~

"For small creatures such as we, the vastness is bearable only through love."
~ Carl Sagan ~

"You have to learn to get up from the table when love is no longer being served."
~ Nina Simone ~

"Love never reasons, but profusely gives; it gives like a thoughtless prodigal its all, and then trembles least it has done too little."
~ Hannah More ~

"Trouble is a part of your life, and if you don't share it, you don't give the person who loves you a chance to love you enough."
~ Dinah Shore ~

"Love is always creative and fear is always destructive."
~ Steve Chandler ~

"You need power, only when you want to do something harmful; otherwise love is enough to get everything done."
~ Charlie Chaplin ~

"Love is a game that two can play and both win."
~ Eva Gabor ~

"It's not who you love. It's how."
~ Ben Affleck ~

"The love we share as mortals may be imperfect, but it still has great power to heal and sustain."
~ Betty J. Eadie ~

"I have decided to stick with love. Hate is too great a burden to bear."
~ Martin Luther King Jr. ~

"Love is not something you have to go looking for when it's where you come from."
~ Anthony Robbins ~

"Any good thing that happens to someone you love can only be good for you too."
~ Rhea Perlman ~

"To me, love has always meant friendship."
~ Jean Harlow ~

"Love becomes help."
~ Paul Tillich ~

Luck

"Luck is everything ... My good luck in life was to be a really frightened person. I'm fortunate to be a coward, to have a low threshold of fear, because a hero couldn't make a good suspense film."
~ Alfred Hitchcock ~

"It wasn't like I ever said, 'I want to be an actor.' I was in the right place at the right time. I went to a local drama group because I found football on the weekends too cold—which is highly ironic because I've had some of the coldest experiences of my life filming *Game of Thrones*."
~ Isaac Hempstead Wright ~

"There are lots of actors out there who are hugely, hugely talented and haven't got the breaks I've had."
~ Kit Harington ~

"There are great actors we'll never see just because they haven't had my luck."
~ Joe Pesci ~

"Luck is the residue of design."
~ John Milton ~

"I find that the harder I work, the more luck I seem to have."
~ Thomas Jefferson ~

"I say luck is when an opportunity comes along
and you're prepared for it."
~ Denzel Washington ~

"Get as much experience as you can, so that you're ready
when luck works. That's the luck."
~ Henry Fonda ~

"I've found that luck is quite predictable. If you want more luck,
take more chances. Be more active. Show up more often."
~ Brian Tracy ~

"The meeting of preparation with opportunity
generates the offspring we call luck."
~ Anthony Robbins ~

"Luck is a dividend of sweat. The more you sweat,
the luckier you get."
~ Ray Kroc ~

"I have only one superstition. I touch all the bases
when I hit a home run."
~ Babe Ruth ~

"The luck of having talent is not enough; one must also
have a talent for luck."
~ Hector Berlios ~

"Luck is for leprechauns"
~ Eric Thomas ~

Marriage

"I hate failure and that divorce was a Number One failure in my eyes. It was the worst period of my life. Neither Desi nor I have been the same since, physically or mentally."
~ Lucille Ball ~

"Have you ever heard of a good marriage growing in front of the cameras?"
~ Brigitte Bardot ~

"I don't meet enough women outside show business, and I wouldn't marry anyone in this field."
~ Paul Lynde ~

"Marriage is a business. A woman cannot combine a career and marriage ... I should not wish to unite the two."
~ Lillian Gish ~

"Women won't let me stay single and I won't let me stay married."
~ Errol Flynn ~

"You only know what happiness is once you're married. But then it's too late."
~ Peter Sellers ~

"A man is not complete until he is married. Then he is finished."
~ Zsa Zsa Gabor ~

"I started off wanting one husband and seven children, but it ended up the other way around."
~ *Lana Turner* ~

"All men make mistakes, but married men find out about them sooner."
~ *Red Skelton* ~

"I guess you could say I have bad taste in men. But I no longer feel the need to be someone's wife."
~ *Halle Berry* ~

"I've never yet met a man who could look after me. I don't need a husband. What I need is a wife."
~ *Joan Collins* ~

"I'm not a real movie star. I've still got the same wife I started out with twenty-eight years ago."
~ *Will Rogers* ~

"Many a man owes his success to his first wife and his second wife to his success."
~ *Jim Backus* ~

"Here in Hollywood you can actually get a marriage license printed on an Etch-A-Sketch."
~ *Dennis Miller* ~

"Marriage requires searing honesty at all costs. I learned that from my third wife."
~ *Alan Arkin* ~

"Conrad Hilton was very generous to me in the divorce settlement. He gave me five thousand Gideon Bibles."
~ Zsa Zsa Gabor ~

"The first time you marry for love, the second for money, and the third for companionship."
~ Jackie Kennedy ~

"Don't marry the person you think you can live with; marry only the individual you think you can't live without."
~ James Dobson ~

"Let any pretty girl announce a divorce in Hollywood and the wolves come running. Fresh meat for the beast, and they are always hungry."
~ Hedy Lamarr ~

"Marriage is a great institution."
~ Elizabeth Taylor ~

"Marriage is forever. It's like cement."
~ Peter O'Toole ~

"Marriage is not a word; it is a sentence."
~ King Vidor ~

"Marriage is the chief cause of divorce."
~ Groucho Marx ~

"Marriage is ridiculous."
~ Goldie Hawn ~

Men and Women

"It sounds trite to go after men who are nice but when you've been hurt a lot it becomes appealing."
~ Salma Hayek ~

"Men learn to love the woman they are attracted to. Women learn to become attracted to the man they fall in love with."
~ Woody Allen ~

"I often wonder whether men and women really suit each other. Perhaps they should live next door and just visit now and then."
~ Katharine Hepburn ~

"I know we have to adjust ourselves as women, and men should have to adjust themselves to a certain degree, too; but, if you still want a man to be a man, you can't adjust him too much. It's like we can never relax as women, and a man can never be the breed that he is."
~ Jacqueline Bisset ~

"Men need to feel important. They feel better when they're with younger girls or unknown girls."
~ Lauren Bacall ~

"Men think about women. Women think about what men think about them."
~ Peter Ustinov ~

"Men like me because I don't wear a brassiere. Women like me because I don't look like a girl who would steal a husband. At least not for long."
~ *Jean Harlow* ~

"Your heart just breaks, that's all. But you can't judge or point fingers. You just have to be lucky enough to find someone who appreciates you."
~ *Audrey Hepburn* ~

"I never meant to be a sexual object for anyone but my husband. I never thought a picture of my body would be tacked up in men's bathrooms. I hate men looking at me and thinking what they think. And I know what they think. They write and tell me."
~ *Lynda Carter* ~

"The reason the all-American boy prefers beauty over brains is that the all-American boy can see better than he can think."
~ *Farrah Fawcett* ~

"Men who love their mothers treat women wonderfully. And they have enormous respect for women."
~ *Ellen Barkin* ~

"I never had a problem resisting somebody that I knew was going to break my heart."
~ *Jennifer Garner* ~

"I'm dating a woman now who, evidently, is unaware of it."
~ *Garry Shandling* ~

"On the one hand, we'll never experience childbirth.
On the other hand, we can open all our own jars."
~ Bruce Willis ~

"There's something real in women's intuition. It's an accurate signpost for decision-making, but it usually bumps up against man's logic. So we have to put ego aside and listen to them."
~ Jon Voight ~

"I think that the day you've figured out the difference between women and men is the day that you're no longer attracted to women. It's the difference that is so fantastic and frustrating and angering and really sexy."
~ Kiefer Sutherland ~

"Most men somewhere in their psyche are still dragging women around by their hair. It's terrible. I have two daughters, but even before my kids were born I always thought that it was terrible."
~ Danny DeVito ~

"It's rare to see women in a film who are not somehow validated by a male or discussing a male or heartbroken by a male, or end up being happy because of a male. It's interesting to think about, and it's very true."
~ Dakota Fanning ~

"Too many women throw themselves into romance because they're afraid of being single, then start making compromises and losing their identity. I won't do that."
~ Julie Delpy ~

"I'm not single, I'm busy. That's my line."
~ Renée Zellweger ~

"A woman has just as much right in this world as a man and can get along in it just as well if she puts her mind to it."
~ Carole Lombard ~

"The world needs strong women. There are a lot of strong women you do not see who are guiding, helping, mothering strong men. They want to remain unseen. It's kind of nice to be able to play a strong woman who is seen."
~ Ginger Rogers ~

"Give me golf clubs, fresh air and a beautiful partner, and you can keep the clubs and the fresh air."
~ Jack Benny ~

"A man can be short and dumpy and getting bald but if he has fire, women will like him."
~ Mae West ~

"If it's true that men are such beasts, this must account for the fact that most women are animal lovers."
~ Doris Day ~

"I liked the fact that Lois was one person with Clark and another with Superman. I think that, as women, we do that a lot when we fall in love."
~ Margot Kidder ~

"If I had as many love affairs as I've been given credit for, I'd be in a jar at the Harvard Medical School."
~ *Frank Sinatra* ~

"Hell, if I'd jumped on all the dames I'm supposed to have jumped on, I'd have had no time to go fishing."
~ *Clark Gable* ~

"In Hollywood you can see things at night that are fast enough to be in the Olympics in the day time."
~ *Will Rogers* ~

"Every time I find a girl who can cook like my mother ... she looks like my father."
~ *Tony Randall* ~

"I've always been the guy who doesn't necessarily get it with women. A woman would have to say, 'I like you, I want to go out with you, you can ask me.' And still I would question it. Did she mean it?"
~ *Kevin James* ~

"I knew right away that Rock Hudson was gay when he did not fall in love with me."
~ *Gina Lollobrigida* ~

"Once a woman has forgiven a man, she must not reheat his sins for breakfast."
~ *Marlene Dietrich* ~

"Your naked body should only belong to those who fall in love with your naked soul."
~ Charlie Chaplin ~

"They can't censor the gleam in my eye."
~ Charles Laughton ~

"When women go wrong, men go right after them."
~ Mae West ~

"What is most beautiful in virile men is something feminine; what is most beautiful in feminine women is something masculine."
~ Susan Sontag ~

"Manly men and womanly women are still here but feeling nervous."
~ Mason Cooley ~

"Even the wisest men make fools of themselves about women, and even the most foolish women are wise about men."
~ Theodor Reik ~

"Smart women love smart men more than smart men love smart women."
~ Natalie Portman ~

"Find me a man who's interesting enough to have dinner with and I'll be happy."
~ Lauren Bacall ~

Mistakes

"The trick to acting is not to be afraid. If you're not afraid of making mistakes, you usually don't make them."
~ Shelley Duvall ~

"A mistake proves somebody stopped talking long enough to do something."
~ John Mason ~

"If you have made mistakes, even serious mistakes, you may have a fresh start any moment you choose, for this thing we call 'failure' is not the falling down, but the staying down."
~ Mary Pickford ~

"Forget mistakes. Forget failures. Forget everything except what you're going to do now and do it. Today is your lucky day."
~ William C. Durant ~

"A person who never made a mistake never tried anything new."
~ Albert Einstein ~

"An expert is a man who has made all the mistakes which can be made in a very narrow field."
~ Niels Bohr ~

"If you aren't making many mistakes, it is a sure sign you are playing it too safe."
~ John Maxwell ~

"The man who makes no mistakes
does not usually make anything."
~ Edward Phelps ~

"Never let any mistake cause you to stop believing in yourself.
Learn from it and go on."
~ Norman Vincent Peale ~

"A poor self-image is the magnifying glass that can transform
a trivial mistake or an imperfection into an overwhelming
symbol of personal defeat."
~ David D. Burns ~

"When things go wrong, don't go with them."
~ Elvis Presley ~

"Mistakes are a part of the dues one pays for a full life."
~ Sophia Loren ~

"Nobody bats 500. We all make mistakes."
~ Desi Arnaz ~

"The greatest mistake you can make in life
is continually fearing that you'll make one."
~ Elbert Hubbard ~

"You make mistakes. Mistakes don't make you."
~ Maxwell Maltz ~

"Look upon the errors of others in sorrow, not in anger."
~ Henry Wadsworth Longfellow ~

Money

"I would roll up pennies to take the subway to work in Times Square. I was broke, but I was happy."
~ Jennifer Garner ~

"There was no sacrifice in acting for me, even when I was starving in New York. I went three days without eating. Charlie Bronson and I sold blood for five dollars so that we could eat."
~ Jack Klugman ~

"I lived below the official American poverty line until I was thirty-one."
~ Dustin Hoffman ~

"There was a time I couldn't get a job."
~ Joe Pesci ~

"I am not biased against the rich because they are rich, but the most lively people are those without money who would like to have some."
~ Errol Flynn ~

"I've been in trouble all my life, I've done the most unutterable rubbish, all because of money. I didn't need it—I've never needed money, even as a child, though I came from a very poor family. But there have been times when the lure of the zeros was simply too great."
~ Richard Burton ~

"A rich man is one who isn't afraid to ask the salesperson to show him something cheaper."
~ Jack Benny ~

"Some day people will learn that material things do not bring happiness and are of little use in making men and women creative and powerful."
~ Mary Pickford ~

"Poverty can teach lessons that privilege cannot."
~ Jack Klugman ~

"If you haven't experienced poverty, you can't imagine it. It's so close, so tight. It's fraught with so much deprivation that it just explodes. Homosexuals, the transgender community, women, blacks—they're mistreated. With poor people, it's not mistreatment. You're not even there. You don't exist. It seeps into your brain."
~ Viola Davis ~

"My parents were very financially challenged. All of us children have the memory of being told that there was no money, we have to sell this, there's no presents for Christmas … of being in the front line of that constant worry, the atmosphere in the home always charged with anxiety. 'What do we do? What do we do?'"
~ Ralph Fiennes ~

"People don't mind if you have a lot of money if they know you're working for it."
~ Jay Leno ~

"Though I am grateful for the blessings of wealth, it hasn't changed who I am. My feet are still on the ground. I'm just wearing better shoes."
~ Oprah Winfrey ~

"Money can't buy happiness. It just helps you look for it in more places."
~ Milton Berle ~

"If it is not to make the world better, what is money for?"
~ Elizabeth Taylor ~

"Philanthropy is almost the only virtue which is sufficiently appreciated by mankind."
~ Henry David Thoreau ~

"I don't think there's anything exceptional or noble in being philanthropic. It's the other attitude that confuses me."
~ Paul Newman ~

"Every man has his price, or a guy like me couldn't exist."
~ Howard Hughes ~

"People who think money will make you happy don't have any."
~ David Geffen ~

"Money can buy you a fine dog, but only love can make him wag his tail."
~ Kinky Friedman ~

"Broke people try to save money.
Wealthy people try to stimulate the economy."
~ *Eric Thomas* ~

"If men did not try and get something for nothing, they might often be able to retain what they have."
~ *Harry Houdini* ~

"I was going to live on my salary or go down swinging."
~ *Gene Tierney* ~

"I was never in it for the money. I was in it just to do it. That's the true pay-off in life. Doing things that you like to do … and then you become pretty good at them."
~ *Johnny Valiant* ~

"Money doesn't make you happy. I now have fifty million dollars but I was just as happy when I had forty-eight million dollars."
~ *Arnold Schwarzenegger* ~

"A rich man is nothing but a poor man with money."
~ *W. C. Fields* ~

"Poverty makes you sad as well as wise."
~ *Bertolt Brecht* ~

"Money dignifies what is frivolous if unpaid for."
~ *Virginia Woolf* ~

"He who wishes to be rich in a day will be hanged in a year."
~ *Leonardo da Vinci* ~

Movies

"Get a director and a writer and leave them alone. That's how the best pictures get made."
~ William Wellman ~

"The first star of a motion picture should be its story."
~ Cecil B. DeMille ~

"Movies are written in sand: applauded today, forgotten tomorrow."
~ D.W. Griffith ~

"A lot of movies are about life, mine are like a slice of cake."
~ Alfred Hitchcock ~

"Each picture has some sort of rhythm which only the director can give it. He has to be like the captain of a ship."
~ Fritz Lang ~

"I've had extraordinary relationships with directors where my opinion is heard, loudly. And they were incredibly collaborative with me. But I believe in the hierarchy of the director. It's their art form and I'm only there to help them achieve it."
~ Nicole Kidman ~

"Filmmaking is a chance to live many lifetimes."
~ Robert Altman ~

"I have always been uncomfortable with a series of movies. I hate that word 'franchise'—it always makes me think of French fries. What I felt each time was that we were going for broke, that this was going to be the last in the series. You can't count on anything."
~ Sigourney Weaver ~

"I look for projects with filmmakers who want to make things that give the audience a fresh experience."
~ Scarlett Johansson ~

"Every movie has a bit of magic in it. Even if it's just for a beat."
~ Sally Hawkins ~

"Not everybody goes to movies to get their life changed."
~ Samuel L. Jackson ~

"It's the movies that have really been running things in America ever since they were invented. They show you what to do, how to do it, when to do it, how to feel about it, and how to look how you feel about it."
~ Andy Warhol ~

"Movies and books open the world for you."
~ Ralph Lauren ~

"Movies are a fad. Audiences really want to see live actors on a stage."
~ Charlie Chaplin ~

"The book is a film that takes place in the mind of the reader. That's why we go to movies and say, 'Oh, the book is better.'"
~ *Paulo Coelho* ~

"You know what your problem is, it's that you haven't seen enough movies—all of life's riddles are answered in the movies."
~ *Steve Martin* ~

"People told me I couldn't kill Nicholson, so I cast him in two roles and killed him off twice."
~ *Tim Burton* ~

"I'm always attracted to lower budget, not because it's lower budget, but because they tend to be better scripts. It's the scripts that tend to be the small arthouse films that tend to be more actor-led and character-driven."
~ *Helena Bonham Carter* ~

"It's hard not to get a big head in the film industry, there are people on a set paid to cater to your every need, from the minute you arrive until you go home. It's kind of strange, but not unpleasant."
~ *Eric Stoltz* ~

"I think one of the things you have to have is a respect for the camera, a real respect, and a real love for it, and to really, when I say take it seriously, quote 'seriously', I mean not patronize it. It's a big mistake to patronize it and think it's a third rate medium, because it's not, it's a great art form."
~ *Anthony Hopkins* ~

"If making movies was easier, there'd be a lot more good movies. So you kind of learn that if it's just a good script, or if it's just a good producer, that's not always enough. You need an entire team of creative people coming together."
~ Chris Evans ~

"I'm a storyteller; that's what exploration really is all about. Going to places where others haven't been and returning to tell a story they haven't heard before."
~ James Cameron ~

"When people ask me if I went to film school, I tell them, 'no, I went to films.'"
~ Quentin Tarantino ~

"Every great film should seem new every time you see it."
~ Roger Ebert ~

"It's not an old movie if you haven't seen it."
~ Lauren Bacall ~

"You hear so much about the old movie moguls and the impersonal factories where there is no freedom. MGM was a wonderful place where decisions were made on my behalf by my superiors. What's wrong with that?"
~ James Stewart ~

"The sound and music are fifty percent of the entertainment in a movie."
~ George Lucas ~

"Nobody knows anything ... not one person in the entire motion picture field knows for a certainty what's going to work. Every time out it's a guess and, if you're lucky, an educated one."
~ William Goldman ~

"You have a bad day at the office, four people know. You suck in a movie, everyone knows."
~ Brad Garrett ~

"A bad play folds and is forgotten, but in pictures we don't bury our dead. When you think it's out of your system, your daughter sees it on television and says, 'My father is an idiot.'"
~ Billy Wilder ~

"Now, more than ever, we need to talk to each other, to listen to each other, and understand how we see the world and cinema is the best medium for doing this."
~ Martin Scorsese ~

"I believe that filmmaking—as, probably, is everything—is a game you should play with all your cards, and all your dice, and whatever else you've got. So, each time I make a movie, I give it everything I have. I think everyone should, and I think everyone should do everything they do that way."
~ Francis Ford Coppola ~

"You can't start a movie by having the attitude that the script is finished, because if you think the script is finished, your movie is finished before the first day of shooting."
~ Steven Spielberg ~

The Mutual Admiration Society

"I just told my agent to forget all other projects for me. I was waiting for Audrey Hepburn. She asked for me, and I was ready. This could be the last and only opportunity I'd have to work with the great and lovely Audrey Hepburn and I was not missing it. Period."
~ *Fred Astaire* ~

"Ingrid Bergman made an enormous impression on me. I couldn't imagine where that kind of acting talent came from."
~ *Grace Kelly* ~

"She was an absolute genius as a comedic actress, with an extraordinary sense for comedic dialogue. It was a God-given gift. Believe me, in the last fifteen years there were ten projects that came to me, and I'd start working on them and I'd think, 'It's not going to work, it needs Marilyn Monroe.' Nobody else is in that orbit; everyone else is earthbound by comparison."
~ *Billy Wilder* ~

"Johnny Cash's legacy, I think if it was one word, it would be 'integrity.' He was the original wild man and grew from that guy that was doing all the crazy things that you read that rock n' rollers do to being someone who was like the father of our country, you know. He was a guest at the White House. He was Billy Graham's friend."
~ *Kris Kristofferson* ~

"I had been a fan of Gene Wilder's for many years, but the first time I saw him in person, my heart fluttered—I was hooked. It felt like my life went from black and white to Technicolor."
~ *Gilda Radner* ~

"I was a 'Laurel and Hardy' nut. I got to know Laurel at the end of his life, and it was a great thrill for me. He left me his bow tie and derby and told me that if they ever made a movie about him, he'd want me to play him."
~ *Dick Van Dyke* ~

"I was lucky enough to make four pictures with Barbara. In the first I turned her in, in the second I killed her, in the third I left her for another woman, and in the fourth I pushed her over a waterfall. The one thing all these pictures had in common was that I fell in love with Barbara Stanwyck—and I did, too."
~ *Fred MacMurray* ~

"I never enjoyed my work more than when I worked with William Powell. He was a brilliant actor, a delightful companion, a great friend and, above all, a true gentleman."
~ *Myrna Loy* ~

"Walter Matthau made all the big money and he was wonderful as Oscar Madison on the stage. You couldn't beat him. I know because I replaced him on Broadway. He was just delightful."
~ *Jack Klugman* ~

"Tony Stark in *Iron Man* helped wider audiences finally embrace the enormous talent of Robert Downey Jr."
~ *Tom Hiddleston* ~

"My skin still crawls if you call me a movie star. I get embarrassed. I think, don't be ridiculous. Maybe it's because I'm British. To me, Julia Roberts—that's a movie star."
~ *Kate Winslet* ~

"In essence, I owe my career to Garry Marshall. There was no known reason for him to hire me for *Pretty Woman*."
~ *Julia Roberts* ~

"I knew Rita Hayworth only enough to know that she was just a tender, sensitive, beautiful human being. A lovely person. Very gentle. She would never stand up for her rights."
~ *Kim Novak* ~

"There's so much emphasis on Daniel Day-Lewis and his process, which is appropriately his own. But I was just blown away by his generosity as an actor. He's so giving as an actor that he just naturally commands the focus on set."
~ *Adam Driver* ~

"I would wish for any one of my colleagues to have the experience of working with Martin Scorsese once in their lifetime."
~ *Daniel Day-Lewis* ~

"Ava Gardner was the most beautiful woman in the world, and it's wonderful that she didn't cut up her face. She addressed aging by picking up her chin and receiving the light in a better way. And she looked like a woman. She never tried to look like a girl."
~ *Sharon Stone* ~

"When I hear the name Michael Jackson, I think of brilliance, of dazzling stars, lasers and deep emotions. I think he is one of the world's biggest and greatest stars, and it just so happens that he is one of the most gifted music makers the world has ever known."

~ Elizabeth Taylor ~

"Elizabeth Taylor is gorgeous, beautiful, and she still is today, I'm crazy about her."

~ Michael Jackson ~

"Cary Grant was wonderful to work with on stage. He would move downstage, so that as he looked at me the audience had to look at me, too. He knew a lot about the theater and how to move around. He was very secure."

~ Fay Wray ~

"He's my favorite! He wrote and produced, and starred in and cast all of his movies! Can you imagine? I get really excited when I talk about Charlie Chaplin."

~ Emma Stone ~

"I look around at my peers, and I'm so blown away by their talent and their beauty and their cool style, as well as their ability to be an actress and be a movie star and be good at it. I mean, they're so good, and we're all trying to get the same parts."

~ Anne Hathaway ~

"I like Christian Bale. I've heard he's a big fan of mine, but I certainly reciprocate. I think he's really very good."

~ Adam West ~

"No one but Gene Tierney could have played *Laura*.
There was no other actress around with her particular
combination of beauty, breeding, and mystery."
~ *Vincent Price* ~

"Someone once said there was a comparison between
Sugar Ray Leonard and Sugar Ray Robinson. Believe me,
there's no comparison. Sugar Ray Robinson was the greatest."
~ *Sugar Ray Leonard* ~

"I want to welcome Jim Varney into a very exclusive club.
That's the Uncle Jed Club. There are hundreds of actors that
have played Hamlet, but only two have played Jed Clampett."
~ *Buddy Ebsen* ~

"James Arness is still my hero. He's a humble and shy guy.
I named my son Matthew after his character. He's a patriotic
American, wounded in World War II. When I painted a portrait
of him, he asked me to make him look like he did on *Gunsmoke*."
~ *Buck Taylor* ~

"One of the greatest gifts to mankind is laughter, and one of
the greatest gifts to laughter is Lucille Ball. God has her now
but thanks to television, we'll have her forever."
~ *Bob Hope* ~

"I'll watch Ricky Gervais in anything he does.
The guy's hilarious."
~ *Danny DeVito* ~

"Sophia Loren would be a glamour girl even if she were in rags selling fish. She has the look, the movement and the intellect."
~ Hedy Lamarr ~

"Oh, how I loved the movies as a little girl. Particularly I loved Yvonnne De Carlo—she was my favorite. Others, too, like Rita Hayworth, but I used to dream that I was Yvonne De Carlo. And I liked that little one—what was her name?—June Allyson, too. But for me there was only one Yvonne De Carlo."
~ Sophia Loren ~

"I will watch everything that Cary Grant did, or Kubrick made, or Bergman."
~ Tim Roth ~

"I became an actor because of Robert DeNiro."
~ Sean Penn ~

"People treat me with a bit too much reverence. Look at Dustin Hoffman. I always envy the way he can speak and be smart and funny and so on. I just can't do that."
~ Robert DeNiro ~

"He was, aside from his acting, a kind of a genius. I'm old enough now to say that I have met a half dozen geniuses. I met Akira Kurasawa. I met Federico Fellini. But Brando was an extraordinary man, possibly number one on a list of geniuses I've had the honor and privilege to meet."
~ Francis Ford Coppola ~

Negativity

"All the people throughout my life who were naysayers pissed me off. But they've all given me a fervor, an angry ambition that cannot be stopped—and I look forward to finding a therapist and working on that."
~ Tobey Maguire ~

"Don't respond to negativity with more negativity. Just put your head down and prove your critics wrong."
~ Frank Sinatra ~

"You get more negative reactions than positive reactions as you go through life, and the big lesson is nobody counts you out but yourself … I never have, I never will."
~ Buddy Ebsen ~

"I know most people always thank people for believing in them. I actually want to thank people that didn't believe in me."
~ Tori Spelling ~

"Don't listen to the nay-sayers. If I would have listened to the nay-sayers, I would still be in the Austrian Alps yodeling."
~ Arnold Schwarzenegger ~

"If I had listened to everyone who told me no, I'd never have gotten anything accomplished. When I really believe in something and someone says, 'You can't do it,' it just spurs me on."
~ Shelley Duvall ~

"I usually don't get too bogged down with my personal problems because that's a one-way street if you get yourself into a negative frame of mind and only see the dark side of life."
~ *Jack Nicholson* ~

"If the world should blow itself up, the last audible voice would be that of an expert saying it can't be done."
~ *Peter Ustinov* ~

"Beware of those who stand aloof and greet each venture with reproof. The world would end if it were run by those who say, 'It can't be done.'"
~ *Samuel Glover* ~

"Other people's views and troubles can be contagious. Don't sabotage yourself by unwittingly adopting negative, unproductive attitudes through your associations with others."
~ *Epictetus* ~

"Most people are fast to stop you before you get started but hesitate to get in the way if you're moving."
~ *Timothy Ferriss* ~

"Without doubt, the most common weakness of all human beings is the habit of leaving their minds open to the negative influence of other people."
~ *Napoleon Hill* ~

"Negatives are like psychic leaches. Negatives get their power from you."
~ *John Kehoe* ~

No Biz Like Show Biz!

"To go into acting is like asking for admission to an insane asylum. Anyone may apply, but only the certifiably insane are admitted."
~ Michael Shurtleff ~

"The sitting around on the set is awful. But I always figure that's what they pay me for. The acting I do for free."
~ Edward G. Robinson ~

"On set I'm an actor like every other actor. Most times, for every part I play, I can think of other actors who would be better. I worry from the moment I take a job."
~ Jack Nicholson ~

"I used to think no one should go into show biz, but now I feel differently. I now feel like it's a great career. If you can do it and make money at it and still not be so famous that you can have a normal life—then I think it's a great career."
~ Julia Sweeney ~

"Everyone should see Hollywood once, I think, through the eyes of a teenage girl who has just passed a screen test."
~ Gene Tierney ~

"You don't retire in this business. You just notice the phone has not rung for ten years."
~ Warren Mitchell ~

"You have to prove you have the goods. People in Hollywood are driven by the heat of success. It's nothing personal. It's not like anyone goes out of his way to screw you. It's just that you have to be the most popular, talented guy in the room at the exact moment they need you."
~ *Jim Carrey* ~

"My agent said, 'You aren't good enough for movies.' I said, 'You're fired.'"
~ *Sally Field* ~

"I was lucky that I made a few movies in a row that people really responded to—not me, particularly, but the films as a whole were appreciated."
~ *Julia Roberts* ~

"Famous people feel that they must perpetually be on the crest of the wave, not realizing that it is against all the rules of life. You can't be on top all the time; it isn't natural."
~ *Olivia de Havilland* ~

"I've always been somewhere down from the top, so I've never had to suffer being knocked off the top."
~ *Harrison Ford* ~

"I recognize that Hollywood is not about seniority. Often it's not even a meritocracy. It's about what you did yesterday. You have a couple of misses, and suddenly it's impossible to find a hit. So the swings are gigantic. But I've always understood it as such, and navigated it as such."
~ *Ben Affleck* ~

"The hardest part of acting is not being guaranteed work. Every job could be your last."
~ *Henry Cavill* ~

"That's how it always is in the entertainment industry, your feet are always treading Jello."
~ *Hedy Lamarr* ~

"I was in this guy's office in L.A. two years ago and he said: 'Love your work, Joe. Love your work.' I'm thinking, wow, he came all the way to catch me as Christ in *Son of Man* at the Barbican. I asked what he'd seen me in and he replied: 'Nothing' … without a flicker of irony.
I thought, Okay, that's how it works."
~ *Joseph Fiennes* ~

"I didn't want to do the obvious role that you see in Hollywood most of the time, which is the heartbroken girl who's waiting to be rescued by the guy, blah, blah, blah. I wanted to do something different."
~ *Gal Gadot* ~

"An actress is not a machine, but they treat you like a machine. A money machine."
~ *Marilyn Monroe* ~

"It's difficult in Hollywood to be allowed to try anything. It's all a terrible compromise. There is no time for art. All that matters is what they call box office."
~ *Greta Garbo* ~

"My TV show had been cancelled. Nothing else had gone anywhere. Some alliances I had made petered out, and nothing came of them, and I was looking at a long, long year ahead of me in which there was no work on the horizon. The phone wasn't ringing. I had two kids, one of them a brand-new baby, and I didn't know if I would be able to keep my house."
~ Tom Hanks ~

"If someone's dumb enough to offer me a million dollars to make a picture, I'm certainly not dumb enough to turn it down."
~ Elizabeth Taylor ~

"I started in movies in 1963, and the first big one was *Rosemary's Baby* in 1967. While you don't notice it right away, it finally dawns on you that eighty percent of the time, you're doing nothing."
~ Charles Grodin ~

"They held up *The Outlaw* for five years. And Howard Hughes had me doing publicity for it every day, five days a week for five years."
~ Jane Russell ~

"If you can believe it, Hollywood wanted to change my birthdate. I was born after Valentine's Day, so they wanted to change it to February 14. A Latin lover should be born on Valentine's Day. I said no."
~ Cesar Romero ~

"I've been fired from every major studio in Hollywood except Disney. They never hired me!"
~ William Wellman ~

"I know my career is going badly because
I'm being quoted correctly."
~ Lee Marvin ~

"I've been told I've done a lot of flop movies. And I think,
'Wow, I've never considered them flops!'
I've loved every character I played."
~ Robin Wright ~

"New York is so full of the best
unemployed actors on the planet."
~ Rachel McAdams ~

"The movie business is based on criminals. Some of them
are in movies and some of them make movies."
~ Daniel Craig ~

"Generally speaking, success brings out
the actors' worst qualities and failure the best."
~ George Abbott ~

"One of my chief regrets during my years in the theater
is that I couldn't sit in the audience and watch me."
~ John Barrymore ~

"There are five stages to an actor's career:
who is Herschel Bernardi? get me Herschel Bernardi;
get me a Herschel Bernardi type; get me a young
Herschel Bernardi; and who is Herschel Bernardi?"
~ Herschel Bernardi ~

Optimism and Pessimism

"Optimism is an intellectual choice."
~ Diana Schneider ~

"One of the things I learned the hard way was that it doesn't pay to get discouraged. Keeping busy and making optimism a way of life can restore your faith in yourself."
~ Lucille Ball ~

"You have to look to the future with optimism instead of negative ideas. Take the good and the bad and face it head on."
~ Goldie Hawn ~

"I am an optimist, without being a Pollyanna. I see the world for what it is, but at the same time I choose to believe in its possibilities. I just always think everything's going to work out. I don't know how it's going to work out, but it is. I've seen that time and time again in my life."
~ Uzo Aduba ~

"I don't believe in pessimism. If something doesn't come up the way you want, forge ahead. If you think it's going to rain, it will."
~ Clint Eastwood ~

"You'll never find a rainbow if you're looking down."
~ Charlie Chaplin ~

"The point of living and of being an optimist is to be foolish enough to believe the best is yet to come."
~ Peter Ustinov ~

"Optimism doesn't wait on facts. It deals with prospects. Pessimism is a waste of time."
~ Norman Cousins ~

"The key to the future of the world is finding the optimistic stories and letting them be known."
~ Pete Seeger ~

"I've never seen a monument erected to a pessimist."
~ Paul Harvey ~

"No one knows enough to be a pessimist."
~ Dr. Wayne Dyer ~

"I find, when you're an optimist, life has a funny way of looking after you."
~ Simon Sinek ~

"An optimist makes the best of it when he gets the worst of it."
~ Henny Youngman ~

"A pessimist is a human joke. We possess such immense resources of power that pessimism is a laughable absurdity."
~ Colin Wilson ~

"When it's dark enough, you can see the stars."
~ Charles A. Beard ~

Opportunities

"I've missed a whole lot of opportunities. A whole lot of them. But I've also caught a lot of them. In the end, it's not about how many I've missed. It's about how many I've caught."
~ Francis Ford Coppola ~

"Your regrets aren't what you did, but what you didn't do. So I take every opportunity."
~ Cameron Diaz ~

"I was smart enough to go through every door that opened."
~ Joan Rivers ~

"I think the young actor who really wants to act will find a way … to keep at it and seize every opportunity that comes along."
~ Sir John Gielgud ~

"You can get digital technology that almost is film quality, and go make little films and do everything you can to find a little understanding of your own voice and it will grow. Don't take no for an answer. Take every opportunity you can to do something."
~ Jon Voight ~

"Hollywood's a mecca, but it's not the final answer. You pick up a camera anyplace in the world, you can make a movie."
~ Robert Duvall ~

"Opportunities multiply as they are seized."
~ Du Mu ~

"We are continually faced by great opportunities
brilliantly disguised as insoluble problems."
~ Lee Iococca ~

"When one door closes, another opens; but we often look
so long and so regretfully upon the closed door
that we do not see the one which has opened for us."
~ Alexander Graham Bell ~

"If the door doesn't open, watch out.
I'm gonna come back and take the hinges off."
~ Les Brown ~

"We often miss opportunity because
it's dressed in overalls and looks like work."
~ Thomas Edison ~

"Opportunity often comes in the form of misfortune
or temporary defeat."
~ Napoleon Hill ~

"I almost feel more anxious lately about, 'Here's your
opportunity, now you've got to make something of it.'"
~ Chris Hemsworth ~

"I wish I had spent less time convinced that I just needed
a break and more time focused on making the most
of the breaks I got."
~ Laura Cayouette ~

Overcoming Your Past

"Regret is useless in life. It's in the past. All we have is now."
~ Marlon Brando ~

"Never regret anything you have done with a sincere affection; nothing is lost that is born of the heart."
~ Basil Rathbone ~

"Nobody cares what you did yesterday. What have you done today to better yourself?"
~ David Goggins ~

"The past cannot be changed. The future is yet in your power."
~ Mary Pickford ~

"You are not your past."
~ Joe Rogan ~

"The past is a guidepost, not a hitching post."
~ L. Thomas Holdcroft ~

"Yesterday ended last night."
~ Zig Ziglar ~

"Don't saw sawdust."
~ Dale Carnegie ~

Patience. Persistence. Perseverance.

"Baby it out. That's an old marble shooter's expression
for approaching your target cautiously instead of
trying to take it out with one shot."
~ Henry Fonda ~

"Sometimes, an indirect route is the quickest way to get there.
Sometimes, you gotta take a little longer to achieve the things
you want to achieve in life. So don't be in a hurry.
Be patient. Be patient."
~ LL Cool J ~

"I've learned that you can get through things that hurt.
Nothing will kill you. Nothing. People are unbelievable.
We have such resilience."
~ Jennifer Aniston ~

"I was determined that with perseverance and faith,
at some point, someone would say, 'This girl has talent,'
and would cast me in something meaningful."
~ Rita Moreno ~

"Perseverance is the hard work you do after you get tired
of doing the hard work you already did."
~ Newt Gingrich ~

"The years teach us what the days can't."
~ Ralph Waldo Emerson ~

"A lot of people give up just before they're about to make it. You know, you never know when that next obstacle is going to be the last one."
~ *Chuck Norris* ~

"Many of life's failures come because we did not realize how close we were to success when we gave up."
~ *Thomas Edison* ~

"Nothing works the first time."
~ *Brian Tracy* ~

"I hated every minute of training, but I said, 'Don't quit. Suffer now and live the rest of your life as a champion.'"
~ *Muhammad Ali* ~

"What I observed about my fellow actors was that most gave up very easily."
~ *Harrison Ford* ~

"I won't quit until I get run over by a truck, a producer or a critic."
~ *Jack Lemmon* ~

"If you hang around long enough, they think you're good. It's either my tenacity or stupidity—I'm not sure which."
~ *Adam West* ~

"I believe in persistence, in leaving no stone unturned, in refusing to be ignored."
~ *Michael Shurtleff* ~

"Perseverance is a great substitute for talent."
~ Steve Martin ~

"It's not that I'm so smart. It's just that I stay with problems longer."
~ Albert Einstein ~

"You just can't beat the person who never gives up."
~ Babe Ruth ~

"Never, never, never give up."
~ Winston Churchill ~

"He conquers who endures."
~ Perseus ~

"I don't believe anything is hard. I just believe you need more practice."
~ Ben Pakulski ~

"To become a champion, fight one more round."
~ James J. Corbett ~

"I am a kind of burr; I shall stick."
~ William Shakespeare ~

"The secret to success is constancy of purpose."
~ Benjamin Disraeli ~

"There will come a time when you believe everything is finished. That will be the beginning."
~ Louis L'Amour ~

Possible vs. Impossible

"Only those who will risk going too far can possibly find out how far one can go."
~ T.S. Eliot ~

"You must do the thing you think you cannot do."
~ Eleanor Roosevelt ~

"If you limit your choice only to what seems possible or reasonable, you disconnect yourself from what you truly want, and all that is left is a compromise."
~ Robert Fritz ~

"Impossible is just a big word thrown around by small men who find it easier to live in the world they've been given than to explore the power they have to change it."
~ Muhammad Ali ~

"Seek the invincible and do the impossible."
~ Fearon Wright ~

"The great pleasure in life is doing what people say you cannot do."
~ Walter Bagehot ~

"The first step is to establish that something is possible, then probability will occur."
~ Elon Musk ~

"We all live so far below the possible level for our lives that when we are set free from the things which hamper us so that we merely approach the potentialities in ourselves, we seem to have been entirely transfigured."
~ Dorothea Brande ~

"Most of the things worth doing in the world had been declared impossible before they were done."
~ Louis D. Brandeis ~

"Impossible is a word to be found only in the dictionary of fools."
~ Napoleon Bonaparte ~

"The only limits in our life are those we impose on ourselves."
~ Bob Proctor ~

"Hard and impossible are two different things."
~ Eric Thomas ~

"What would you attempt to do if you knew you would not fail?"
~ Dr. Robert Schuller ~

"Act as if it were impossible to fail."
~ Dorothea Brande ~

"Being realistic is the most common path to mediocrity."
~ Will Smith ~

"Attempt the impossible in order to improve your work."
~ Brian Tracy ~

"Nothing is impossible.
Some things are just less likely than others."
~ Jonathan Winters ~

"Practice even what seems impossible."
~ Marcus Aurelius ~

"Successful and unsuccessful people do not vary greatly in their abilities. They vary in their desires to reach their potential."
~ John Maxwell ~

"Men are generally idle, and ready to satisfy themselves,
and intimidate the industry of others,
by calling that impossible which is only difficult."
~ Samuel Johnson ~

"Determine that the thing can and shall be done,
and then we shall find the way."
~ Abraham Lincoln ~

"Most things are not obtained simply because
they are not attempted."
~ Balthasar Gracian ~

"It is our duty as men and women to proceed as though the limits of our abilities do not exist."
~ Pierre Teilhard de Chardin ~

"Knock the 't' off the 'can't'."
~ George Reeves ~

Preparation and Rehearsal

"Fortune favors the prepared."
~ Howard Hawks ~

"Begin to be now what you will be hereafter."
~ William James ~

"The will to succeed is important, but what's more important is the will to prepare."
~ Bobby Knight ~

"Preparation and research is a privilege: I love to do it, I'm very inquisitive. I also know the more work I put into the character, the more apparent it'll be on the screen."
~ Russell Crowe ~

"I fear other actors who are not prepared. And I fear directors who are afraid."
~ Tommy Lee Jones ~

"I never prepare. I think that's completely overrated. It's a very simple job. All you have to do is hit this bright mark, stand in the right spot and say the line. So I don't really believe in preparation."
~ Joaquin Phoenix ~

"All the real work is done in the rehearsal period."
~ Donald Pleasence ~

"Something I learned as an actor was which scenes needed to be rehearsed and which actors are good with rehearsal, which actors learn from it, and which ones grow stale because they start to second-guess themselves."
~ Angelina Jolie ~

"The more takes I do, the worse I get."
~ Richard Widmark ~

"Garbo went through a great deal to get a scene right. She worked out every gesture in advance and learned every syllable of dialogue exactly as written. She never improvised and I respected her for that."
~ George Cukor ~

"I was lazy. I would have been a hell of a lot better actress had I taken it more seriously. I never had the proper respect for acting. Quite often, I learned my lines on the way to the studio."
~ Ava Gardner ~

"When you are not practicing, remember, someone somewhere is practicing, and when you meet him he will win."
~ Bill Bradley ~

"You might have, as a character, 30 pages of dialogue a day if you're what they call a 'front-burner story.' So you go home, you learn your lines for the next day, you get up, you're there at 7 in the morning, you do a quick rehearsal, you're on camera, you might leave, you know, at 7 at night and start the whole thing over again."
~ Julianne Moore ~

Purpose and Fulfillment

"To me, if you love it enough to devote your life to it, then you're doing the right thing."
~ Kris Kristofferson ~

"Every script I've written and every series I've produced have expressed the things I most deeply believe."
~ Michael Landon ~

"This is the real secret of life—to be completely engaged with what you are doing in the here and now. And instead of calling it work, realize it is play."
~ Alan Watts ~

"I wasn't trying to be rich or famous; I was trying to figure out what is this thing in me that won't let me sleep, that makes me restless and makes me keep pushing. I was trying to discover who I was."
~ T.D. Jakes ~

"It was only when I realized how actors have the power to move people that I decided to pursue acting as a career."
~ Cate Blanchett ~

"I think an artist's responsibility is more complex than people realize."
~ Jodie Foster ~

"My lifetime dream has been to assemble and preserve the history of the Hollywood film industry."
~ Debbie Reynolds ~

"I personally believe that each of us was put here for a purpose—to build not to destroy."
~ Red Skelton ~

"A film without a message is just a waste of time."
~ D.W. Griffith ~

"I stopped making films to look after animals."
~ Brigitte Bardot ~

"I stayed in show business to pay for my animal business."
~ Betty White ~

"Act as if what you do makes a difference. It does."
~ William James ~

"Seems like when we cease to inspire … we cease."
~ Kirstie Alley ~

"Do something worth remembering."
~ Elvis Presley ~

"When you discover your mission, you will feel its demand. It will fill you with enthusiasm and a burning desire to get to work on it."
~ W. Clement Stone ~

Rejection

"You have to learn to take rejection not as an indication of personal failing but as a wrong address."
~ *Ray Bradbury* ~

"I was up for a great part but they told me, 'Sorry, you're the best actor but this part calls for a guy-next-door type. You don't look as if you've ever lived next door to anyone.'"
~ *Donald Sutherland* ~

"As a teenager, my favorite rejection was, 'She looks too healthy,' which of course translates as, 'She needs to lose weight.'"
~ *Christina Ricci* ~

"Instead of feeling rejected, know that you're being protected."
~ *Kimberly Bliquez* ~

"You have to dream, you have to have a vision, and you have to set a goal for yourself that might even scare you a little because sometimes that seems far beyond your reach. Then I think you have to develop a kind of resistance to rejection, and to the disappointments that are sure to come your way."
~ *Gregory Peck* ~

"Some actors couldn't figure out how to withstand the constant rejection. They couldn't see the light at the end of the tunnel."
~ *Harrison Ford* ~

"The truth is I love the insecurity part of it. It keeps me on my toes. I think you become bland and predictable without the stress and angst. There's a certain lethargy that sets in."
~ Liam Neeson ~

"Actors search for rejection. If they don't get it, they reject themselves."
~ Charlie Chaplin ~

"I take rejection as someone blowing a bugle in my ear to wake me up and get going, rather than retreat."
~ Sylvester Stallone ~

"If I spend all my time being upset about having lost a job, then the next however many auditions I have are going to be useless."
~ Henry Cavill ~

"I don't think actors should ever expect to get a role, because the disappointment is too great. You've got to think of things as an opportunity. An audition's an opportunity to have an audience."
~ Al Pacino ~

"I wasn't smart enough to be discouraged. I keep saying that and I don't think anybody really understands or believes it … I didn't ever think about doing anything else. I wasn't prepared to do anything else. I hadn't any talent to do anything else."
~ Henry Fonda ~

"You get used to the rejection and you don't take it personally."
~ Daniel Craig ~

"Desperation is the perfume of the young actor. It's so satisfying to have gotten rid of it. If you keep smelling it, it can drive you crazy. In this business, a lot of people go nuts, go eccentric, even end up dead from it. Not my plan."
~ Uma Thurman ~

"I really wish I was less of a thinking man and more of a fool not afraid of rejection."
~ Billy Joel ~

"Go where you are loved. People who see the best in you bring out the best in you.
~ Lupita Nyong'o ~

"Go where you're celebrated, not tolerated."
~ Sammy Maloof ~

"For every successful actor or actress, there are countless numbers who don't make it. The name of the game is rejection. You go to an audition and you're told you're too tall or you're too Irish or your nose is not quite right. You're rejected for your education, you're rejected for this or that and it's really tough."
~ Liam Neeson ~

"Look up the definition of rejection in the dictionary, get really comfortable with it, and then maybe you can go into acting."
~ Loni Anderson ~

"Rejection is good for the soul."
~ Eva Mendes ~

Risk

"I've always been very competitive, and a part of that is pushing your boundaries—taking a risk and being able to live with the loss that comes with taking a risk."
~ Scarlett Johansson ~

"The thing to do is to keep taking chances. If you're going to learn anything, you've got to learn from the masters. Plus you've got to work with the talented beginner too."
~ Charles Durning ~

"Nothing in life is worthwhile unless you take risks. Fall forward. Every failed experiment is one step closer to success."
~ Denzel Washington ~

"There are many talented people who haven't fulfilled their dreams because they over thought it, or they were too cautious, and were unwilling to make the leap of faith."
~ James Cameron ~

"The chief danger in life is that you may take too many precautions."
~ Alfred Adler ~

"If something's important enough, you should try even if the probable outcome is failure."
~ Elon Musk ~

Scripts

"Writing is the life blood of everything in Hollywood. Without writers, there are no scripts, no acting work."
~ Ali Wong ~

"I think you have to look at screenwriting as an art form because it's not all that easy to do. Not all that many people can do it. So you have to go out and find the material, or develop it from scratch, and I'm one of the handful of people who actually spends his own money on developing and producing projects I like."
~ Kevin Costner ~

"The best script in the world doesn't work perfectly when you actually act it out. That's a law. That's a given. So you have to play with everything. And the more fun you have with it, the better the finished product."
~ Ricky Gervais ~

"Good writing will bring you to places you don't even expect sometimes."
~ James Gandolfini ~

"I'm most suspicious of scripts that have a lot of stage direction at the top of the page … sunrise over the desert and masses of … a whole essay before you get to the dialogue."
~ Anthony Hopkins ~

"I read a lot of scripts and so many are clearly a knockoff of one familiar genre or another."
~ Edward Norton ~

"I see a lot of scripts, and very few of them leap off the page at you."
~ Sam Shepard ~

"Most of the scripts that land on my desk are stuff you read and go, 'Is someone really gonna make this?'"
~ Jason Statham ~

"I've been fortunate. I don't pick scripts. Scripts pick me."
~ Denzel Washington ~

"I want to aspire to something like what Denzel Washington does, which is try to find scripts written for white actors—or Jodie Foster, who reads scripts for male actors."
~ Wentworth Miller ~

"The best thing for me is, when I'm not working, is to be at home and to have a script or two scripts is better, and to be just walking around the house and just thinking about the lines."
~ Christopher Walken ~

"I try to read everything that's sent me—play scripts, movie scripts—but I've had to make a rule. If the author hasn't grabbed me by page twenty-five, the piece goes back with a note of apology."
~ Hume Cronyn ~

"My own mentality is that I've retired. They send me these scripts and if I absolutely have to do it, then I go to work."
~ Michael Caine ~

"I knew what my scripts would say before I opened them: 'Enter Conchita.' I played handmaidens, Indian squaws, and Mexican dancers."
~ Rita Moreno ~

"The multilevel, the conscious and the unconscious, is natural when I write scripts, when I come up with ideas and stories."
~ Bong Joon-ho ~

"The goal is always to do B material in an A fashion."
~ J. J. Abrams ~

"I think the best-written films or television series have a measure of the opposite of what they are."
~ Bryan Cranston ~

"You won't find me in a romantic comedy. Those movies don't speak to me. People don't come to talk to me about those scripts, because they probably think I'm this dark, twisted, miserable person."
~ Naomi Watts ~

"I've got a big closet of scripts, and a big stack of scripts on the side of my desk, because you get a whole bunch. Nothing's going to be perfect, and I realize that; but I am a perfectionist, so you go through a lot of stuff."
~ Chris Tucker ~

Self-Awareness and Self-Reflection

"We know what we are, but not what we may be."
~ William Shakespeare ~

"The world is full of magical things patiently waiting for our wits to grow sharper."
~ Bertrand Russell ~

"I sometimes truly despair at ever being meaningfully altered and affected by the things I claim are so important to me."
~ Olympia Dukakis ~

"I've never felt completely satisfied with what I've done. I tend to see things too critically. I'm trying to get over that. I've got the Jewish guilt and the Irish shame and it's a hell of a job distinguishing which is which."
~ Kevin Kline ~

"I spend half my time just living my life, and the other half analyzing it."
~ David Schwimmer ~

"I was a strange kid. I never really fit in. I was never comfortable in my own skin because I was a giant kid with no athletic ability."
~ Brad Garrett ~

"Self-awareness is a key to self-mastery."
~ Gretchen Rubin ~

"I have a dread of being considered bland, but I've had
to reconcile myself to the fact that that's what I am."
~ George Segal ~

"I think I may have become an actor to hide from myself.
You can escape into a character."
~ John Candy ~

"There are two ways to be cool: One is to be disinterested and make it seem like you must be doing something much more interesting than everybody else if you are this disinterested. The other is to be extremely interested. You are not trying to please anyone, but you are really invested *and* are really focused."
~ Maggie Gyllenhaal ~

"I knew I belonged to the public and to the world, not because I was talented or even beautiful, but because I had never belonged to anything or anyone else."
~ Marilyn Monroe ~

"What a wonderful life I've had.
I only wish I'd realized it sooner."
~ Sidonie-Gabrielle Colette ~

"It is sometimes expedient to forget who we are."
~ Publilius Syrus ~

"You have to know that your real home is within."
~ Quincy Jones ~

Self-Confidence

"You have to feel confident. If you don't, then you're going to be hesitant and defensive, and there'll be a lot of things working against you."
~ *Clint Eastwood* ~

"I've always had confidence. Before I was famous, that confidence got me into trouble. After I got famous, it just got me into more trouble."
~ *Bruce Willis* ~

"If I have lost confidence in myself, I have the universe against me."
~ *Ralph Waldo Emerson* ~

"Confidence is not a personality trait. It's actually the ability to go from thought into action."
~ *Mel Robbins* ~

"There never was a winner that didn't expect to win in advance."
~ *Denis Waitley* ~

"If you are insecure, guess what? The rest of the world is, too. Do not overestimate the competition and underestimate yourself. You are better than you think."
~ *Timothy Ferriss* ~

"All confidence is acquired. No one is born with confidence."
~ David J. Schwartz ~

"I'd be conceited if I said I could,
but I'd be lying if I said I couldn't."
~ Rocky Marciano ~

"I believe in me. I'm a little screwed up but I'm beautiful."
~ Steve McQueen ~

"You are an answer. Walk like it. Talk like it. Plan like it."
~ T. D. Jakes ~

"You don't have to be perfect to be confident."
~ Stuart Wilde ~

"Life is not easy for any of us. But what of that?
We must have perseverance and above all confidence in ourselves. We must believe that we are gifted for something, and that this thing, at whatever cost, must be attained."
~ Marie Curie ~

"Confidence is everything in this business."
~ Reese Witherspoon ~

"Underconfidence breeds underachievement."
~ Lou Holtz ~

"Confidence is essential, but ego is not."
~ Sam Mendes ~

Self-Development and Self-Realization

"Everybody talks about wanting to change things and help and fix, but ultimately all you can do is fix yourself. And that's a lot. Because if you can fix yourself, it has a ripple effect."
~ Rob Reiner ~

"The butterfly does not look back at the caterpillar in shame, just as you should not look back at your past in shame. Your past was part of your transformation."
~ Anthony Gucciardi ~

"I always wanted to be someone better the next day than I was the day before."
~ Sidney Poitier ~

"Tomorrow hopes we have learned something from yesterday."
~ John Wayne ~

"Life is not a having and a getting, but a being and a becoming."
~ Myrna Loy ~

"Perfection is not attainable, but if we chase perfection we can catch excellence."
~ Vince Lombardi ~

"I became great by being good over a long period of time."
~ John Elway ~

"It's better to hang out with people better than you.
Pick out associates whose behavior is better than yours
and you'll drift in that direction."
~ Warren Buffett ~

"I think it's very important to have a feedback loop,
where you're constantly thinking about what you've done
and how you could be doing it better."
~ Elon Musk ~

"Only I can change my life. No one can do it for me."
~ Carol Burnett ~

"Let the refining and the improving of your own life keep you
so busy that you have little time to criticize others."
~ H. Jackson Browne ~

"Think bigger. Forget limits. Embrace the idea
of endless possibility. It will change you."
~ Marianne Williamson ~

"If they can make penicillin out of moldy bread,
they can sure make something out of you."
~ Muhammad Ali ~

"What we achieve inwardly will change our outer reality."
~ Plutarch ~

"So much of what you are not is because you are literally
standing in your own way of becoming."
~ Leo Buscaglia ~

Self-Esteem

"Better see yourself clean and bright; you are the window through which you must see the world."
~ George Bernard Shaw ~

"I still think people will find out that I'm really not very talented. I'm really not very good. It's all just been a big sham."
~ Michelle Pfeiffer ~

"Respect your efforts, respect yourself. Self-respect leads to self-discipline. When you have both firmly under your belt, that's real power."
~ Clint Eastwood ~

"High self-esteem isn't a luxury. It's a necessity for anyone who has important goals to achieve."
~ Jack Canfield ~

"If you're self-compassionate, you'll tend to have higher self-esteem than if you're endlessly self-critical. And like high self-esteem—self-compassion is associated with significantly less anxiety and depression, as well as more happiness, optimism, and positive emotions."
~ David D. Burns ~

"If you can't stand yourself, neither can anybody else."
~ Sid Caesar ~

"You can even say that I hated myself at certain periods. I was too fat, or maybe too tall, or maybe just plain too ugly … you can say my definiteness stems from underlying feelings of insecurity and inferiority. I couldn't conquer these feelings by acting indecisive. I found the only way to get the better of them was by adopting a forceful, concentrated drive."
~ Audrey Hepburn ~

"I don't think being the only child of a single parent helped. I was always a little unsteady in my self-belief. Then there was the Jewish thing. I love being Jewish, I have no problem with it at all. But it did become like a scar, with all these people saying you don't look it."
~ Lauren Bacall ~

"When a kid didn't have any love when he was small, he begins to wonder if he's good enough. You know if my mother didn't love me, and I didn't have a father, I mean, well, I guess I'm not very good."
~ Steve McQueen ~

"The strongest factor for success is self-esteem: Believing you can do it, believing you deserve it, believing you will get it."
~ John Assaraf ~

"I think high self-esteem is overrated. A little low self-esteem is actually quite good. Maybe you're not the best, so you should work a little harder."
~ Jay Leno ~

"Until you value yourself, you won't value your time.
Until you value your time, you will not do anything with it."
~ M. Scott Peck ~

"I was once afraid of people saying, "Who does she think she is?"
Now I have the courage to stand and say, 'This is who I am.'"
~ Oprah Winfrey ~

"When everyone has high expectation for you
it can attack your insecurities."
~ Bryan Cranston ~

"Love yourself first and everything else falls into line. You really
have to love yourself to get anything done in this world."
~ Lucille Ball ~

"Self esteem in the belief that you can handle life."
~ Trevor Moawad ~

"It's not your job to like me, it's mine."
~ Byron Katie ~

"What would you be like if you were the only person in the
world? If you want to be truly happy you must be that person."
~ Quentin Crisp ~

"We have to learn to be our own best friends because we fall
too easily into the trap of being our own worst enemies."
~ Roderick Thorp ~

Self-Reliance

"Sometimes if you want to see a change for the better,
you have to take things into your own hands."
~ Clint Eastwood ~

"I believe you make your day. You make your life. So much of it
is all perception, and this is the form that I built for myself.
I have to accept it and work within those compounds,
and it's up to me."
~ Brad Pitt ~

"I always knew there wasn't going to be anybody to help me
and emotionally support me, that whatever I did
I'd have to do on my own."
~ Jack Nicholson ~

"You learn to cope with whatever you have to cope with.
I spent my childhood in New York, riding on subways and
buses. And you know what you learn if you're a New Yorker?
The world doesn't owe you a damn thing."
~ Lauren Bacall ~

"If your ship doesn't come in, swim out to it."
~ Jonathan Winters ~

"If your ship has not yet come in, build a lighthouse."
~ Rod R. Garcia ~

"If opportunity doesn't knock, build a door."
~ *Milton Berle* ~

"Once a person is determined to help themselves, there is nothing that can stop them."
~ *Nelson Mandela* ~

"It is better to be a lion for a day than a sheep all your life."
~ *Elizabeth Kenny* ~

"I'm a fighter and not a victim. Think of yourself and make the most of life."
~ *Jill Ireland* ~

"You have to be the hero of your own story."
~ *Joe Rogan* ~

"You must become the answer to your own prayer for change in the world."
~ *Myles Munroe* ~

"Fate knows where you are going, but it is up to you to drive there."
~ *Michelle Keesling* ~

"The best way to predict the future is to create it."
~ *Abraham Lincoln* ~

"The best place to find a helping hand is at the end of your own arm."
~ *Swedish Proverb* ~

Service

"Service to others is the rent you pay for your room here on earth."
~ Muhammad Ali ~

"You feel alive to the degree that you feel you can help others."
~ John Travolta ~

"If the world seems cold to you, kindle fires to warm it."
~ Lucy Larcom ~

"Instead of cursing the darkness, light a candle."
~ Benjamin Franklin ~

"Work is life for me, it is the only point of life—and with it there is almost religious belief that service is everything."
~ Laurence Olivier ~

"The most important thing in anyone's life is to be giving something. The quality I can give is fun, joy and happiness. This is my gift."
~ Ginger Rogers ~

"Is there any real purpose in being alive if all we are going to do is get up every day and live only for ourselves? Live your life to help others. Give and live selflessly."
~ Joyce Meyer ~

"Being in service and being involved in something that is greater than you is what makes a person complete and whole. The very first thing I ever did in terms of activism was for an anti-atom bomb rally."
~ Rita Moreno ~

"How can I be useful, of what service can I be? There is something inside me, what can it be?"
~ Vincent van Gogh ~

"If one is lucky, a solitary fantasy can totally transform one million realities."
~ Maya Angelou ~

"Every Friday, I used to have about fifty, sixty kids who would wait for me on Sunset Boulevard and I'd take them all to dinner. All runaways."
~ Al Lewis ~

"When you're not thinking about yourself, you're usually happy."
~ Al Pacino ~

"Always help someone. You might be the only one who does."
~ Muriel Strode ~

"There is not a moment without some duty."
~ Cicero ~

"Love grows by service."
~ Charlotte Perkins Gilman ~

Simplicity

"I find that kid actors are great reminders of the simplicity of acting. As you get older, you can sometimes complicate things a little more. You can become too aware of, 'Okay, this is the scene emotionally. This is where we need to be. We've got the climax coming up.' You can start to analyze it too much."

~ Hugh Jackman ~

"Things that I grew up with stay with me. You start a certain way, and then you spend your whole life trying to find a certain simplicity that you had. It's less about staying in childhood than keeping a certain spirit of seeing things in a different way."

~ Tim Burton ~

"The more there is, the less I want. The more man flies to the moon, the more I want to look at a tree."

~ Audrey Hepburn ~

"There seems to be some perverse human characteristic that likes to make easy things difficult."

~ Warren Buffett ~

"Real art is basic emotion. If a scene is handled with simplicity—and I don't mean simple—it'll be good, and the public will know it."

~ John Wayne ~

"Art, it seems to me, should simplify."

~ Willa Cather ~

"Unnecessary possessions are unnecessary burdens.
If you have them, you have to take care of them!
There is great freedom in simplicity of living. It is those
who have enough but not too much who are the happiest."
~ Peace Pilgrim ~

"I like simplicity; I don't need luxury."
~ Francis Ford Coppola ~

"Making films is like making stuff together as kids."
~ Sofia Coppola ~

"Truth is ever to be found in simplicity,
and not in the multiplicity and confusion of things."
~ Isaac Newton ~

"Simplicity in character, in manners, in style;
in all things the supreme excellence is simplicity."
~ Henry Wadsworth Longfellow ~

"Complexity is the enemy of execution."
~ Anthony Robbins ~

"Misery is complexity. Happiness is simplicity."
~ Lester Levenson ~

"Out of clutter, find simplicity."
~ Albert Einstein ~

"If you can't write your idea on the back of my calling card,
you don't have a clear idea."
~ David Belasco ~

Solitude

"Cultivate solitude and quiet and a few sincere friends, rather than mob merriment, noise and thousands of nodding acquaintances."
~ William Powell ~

"There is a need for aloneness, which I don't think most people realize for an actor. It's almost having certain kinds of secrets for yourself that you'll let the whole world in on only for a moment, when you're acting. But everybody is always tugging at you. They'd all like sort of a chunk of you."
~ Marilyn Monroe ~

"There's a difference between solitude and loneliness. I can understand the concept of being a monk for a while."
~ Tom Hanks ~

"I'm used to living alone, and I like it that way. You become so selfish living alone … I'd make a terrible husband anyway."
~ Paul Lynde ~

"Loneliness is the universal problem of rich people."
~ Joan Collins ~

"Solitude scares me. It makes me think about love, death, and war. I need distraction from anxious, black thoughts."
~ Brigitte Bardot ~

"Let's face it. I'm a person that feels pretty alienated from the rest of the world and never felt understood by anyone."
~ *Sean Penn* ~

"When things are going well, I like to have people to share it with. I've been alone in troubled times, and I don't mind that. Some things have to be endured alone. As Hemingway said, the human being is strong in all the broken places."
~ *Susan Sarandon* ~

"People are always so boring when they band together. You have to be alone to develop all the idiosyncrasies that make a person interesting."
~ *Andy Warhol* ~

"The monotony and solitude of a quiet life stimulates the creative mind."
~ *Albert Einstein* ~

"It's a lovely experience walking around a museum by yourself."
~ *Brad Pitt* ~

"I love walking in the woods, on the trails, along the beaches. I love being part of nature. I love walking alone. It is therapy. One needs to be alone, to recharge one's batteries."
~ *Grace Kelly* ~

"What a lovely surprise to finally discover how unlonely being alone can be."
~ *Ellen Burstyn* ~

Staying on Track

"Even if you're on the right track, if you just sit still you'll get run over."
~ Will Rogers ~

"We need to learn to set our course by the stars, not by the lights of every passing ship."
~ General Omar Bradley ~

"Be not afraid of growing slowly; be afraid only of standing still."
~ Chinese Proverb ~

"The road to success is dotted with many tempting parking spaces."
~ Will Rogers ~

"There are no short cuts to any place worth going."
~ Beverly Sills ~

"I don't know anybody's road who's been paved perfectly for them. There are no manuals. You don't know what life has in store for you."
~ Drew Barrymore ~

"Find your joy in something finished, not in a thousand things begun."
~ Douglas Mallock ~

Study

"I do not read a book; I hold a conversation with the author."
~ Elbert Hubbard ~

"My mother brought us to the library every week, and I read a lot. That's what kept me company. I went from school to school, but there was always reading."
~ Julianne Moore ~

"The public library is more than a repository of books. It's a mysterious, wondrous place with the power to change lives."
~ Elizabeth Taylor ~

"I learned how to read in second grade, and I entered a summer contest at my local library in Chattanooga, Tennessee. If you read more books than anybody else, you got your Polaroid up on the bulletin board, and I did."
~ Frances McDormand ~

"It's a poor student who isn't the equal of his teacher."
~ Lou Thesz ~

"Always stay a student."
~ Frank Shamrock ~

"An investment in knowledge always pays the best interest."
~ Benjamin Franklin ~

"Turn your automobile into a university on wheels."
~ Earl Nightingale ~

"If people knew how hard I worked to achieve my mastery, it wouldn't seem so wonderful after all."
~ Michelangelo ~

"We do not rise to the level of our expectations. We fall to the level of our training."
~ Archilochus ~

"My goal was not to be famous or rich but to be good at what I did. And that required going to New York and studying and working in the theater."
~ Shirley Knight ~

"The beautiful thing about learning is that no one can take it away from you."
~ B.B. King ~

"Conversation enriches the understanding, but solitude is the school of genius."
~ Edward Gibbon ~

"Live as if you were to die tomorrow. Learn as if you were to live forever."
~ Mahatma Gandhi ~

"You cannot afford to confine your studies to the classroom. The universe and all of history is your classroom."
~ Stella Adler ~

Success

"Success is not the result of spontaneous combustion. You must set yourself on fire."
~ *Reggie Leach* ~

"A person can succeed at almost anything for which he has unlimited enthusiasm."
~ *Charles Schwab* ~

"A great secret of success is to go through life as a man who never gets used up."
~ *Dr. Albert Schweitzer* ~

"Aim for success, not perfection. Never give up your right to be wrong, because then you will lose the ability to learn new things and move forward with your life."
~ *Dr. David M. Burns* ~

"Failure has a thousand explanations. Success doesn't need one."
~ *Alec Guinness* ~

"My mother drew a distinction between achievement and success. She said that 'achievement is the knowledge that you have studied and worked hard and done the best that is in you. Success is being praised by others, and that's nice, too, but not as important or satisfying. Always aim for achievement and forget about success.'"
~ *Helen Hayes* ~

"Successful people are always survival testimonies."
~ Dr. Myles Munroe ~

"I can give you a six-word formula for success:
Think things through—then follow through."
~ Captain Edward Rickenbacker ~

"Success usually comes to those
who are too busy to be looking for it."
~ Henry David Thoreau ~

"A champion is afraid of losing.
Everyone else is afraid of winning."
~ Billie Jean King ~

"Don't let your successes go to your head,
and don't let your failures go to your heart."
~ Will Smith ~

"I'm a success today because I had a friend who believed in me
and I didn't have the heart to let him down."
~ Abraham Lincoln ~

"Success is a beast. And it actually puts the emphasis on the
wrong thing. You get away with more instead of looking within."
~ Brad Pitt ~

"I couldn't wait for success, so I went ahead without it."
~ Jonathan Winters ~

Survival Jobs

"Do what you have to do, to do what you want to do."
~ Denzel Washington ~

"So many of my friends have been like, "Oh I'm not allowed to go off and do that cause I need to get a 'Plan B.' And I understand that, but we spend so much time trying to figure out our 'Plan B' that we never really fully pursue our 'Plan A.'"
~ Maisie Williams ~

"I enjoyed carpentry, and it was very good to me for twelve years."
~ Harrison Ford ~

"Your profession is not what brings home your weekly paycheck, your profession is what you're put here on Earth to do, with such passion and such intensity that it becomes spiritual in nature."
~ Vincent van Gogh ~

"When I was twenty-one years old, I had a job playing Santa Claus in a shopping center in Sacramento. I was rail thin, so it's not like I was a traditional Santa Claus even then. I had a square stomach; that was the shape of the sofa cushion that I had stuffed into my pants."
~ Tom Hanks ~

"I had a job once selling encyclopedias, and that was an interesting job because I learned a lot about people's vulnerabilities and how salesmen take advantage of them."

~ *Jon Voight* ~

"I was living in a small town in Indiana working as a telemarketer and a vacuum salesman. I was really bad; the vacuums seemed to always be falling apart. Every time I did a demonstration, I'd say, 'This is the material the astronauts used on Apollo 13.' And no sooner had that come out of my mouth, something would malfunction."

~ *Adam Driver* ~

"If the acting thing hadn't worked out for me, I'd be laying phone cable in northern Ontario."

~ *Kiefer Sutherland* ~

"I got fired when I was a dishwasher at Denny's. That set me back a little bit. You don't realize how important dishwashers are until you do the job."

~ *Kelsey Grammar* ~

"I had a lot of survival jobs. One was for the Witty Ditty singing-telegram company. I was in the red-and-white stripes with the straw boater hat and kazoo. Balloons. Even when you're sleeping on a friend's couch, you have to pay some kind of rent."

~ *Aaron Sorkin* ~

"Selling tickets at the Bing Theater at LACMA was my first job in L.A."

~ *Elvis Mitchell* ~

"I have a secret admiration for insurance salesmen, doormen, taxi drivers, guys working on the Alaska pipeline ... many hundreds of jobs where they work. There's lots of jobs now in the world where we don't work, we push a button. I don't work. I've never worked. I take great pride in the fact that I played baseball, I drove race cars, I drove racing boats, I flew airplanes and I acted. None of those things are work. Doing what you want to do, that's not work."
~ Kurt Russell ~

"For eight years I did effects for other movies until I got my movie made."
~ Guillermo del Toro ~

"After my last audition for Game of Thrones, they said, 'Congratulations, Princess.' I was like, 'Bye-bye, call centre.'"
~ Emilia Clarke ~

"I was the music director at a dinner theater called the 'Pheasant Run Theater' in the suburbs of Chicago, and that was my side gig while I acted."
~ Sean Hayes ~

"I worked at Deutsche Bank for about eight years on their overnight shift. I was working consistently in the theater. I just wanted to know that my rent was going to be paid on time!"
~ Chandra Wilson ~

"Your job is what they pay you to do. Your work is what you were born to do."
~ Myles Munroe ~

Taking Small Steps Daily

"If you can't feed a hundred people, then feed just one."
~ *Mother Teresa* ~

"The person who removes a mountain begins
by carrying away small stones."
~ *Anonymous* ~

"I do small things. I try to do good things every day."
~ *Jackie Chan* ~

"Step by step and the thing is done."
~ *Charles Atlas* ~

"It's better to move forward at a snail's pace,
than backward at any pace."
~ *Rhonda Begos* ~

"A man can do only what he can do. But if he does that
each day he can sleep at night and do it again the next day."
~ *Albert Schweitzer* ~

"You'll never win your war by running from your battles."
~ *Trent Shelton* ~

"Don't ever underestimate the utility
of incremental improvement."
~ *Jordan Peterson* ~

"Everyone is trying to accomplish something big,
not realizing that life is made up of little things."
~ Frank A. Clark ~

"I long to accomplish a great and noble task, but it is my chief duty to accomplish small tasks as if they were great and noble."
~ Helen Keller ~

"People seldom see the halting and painful steps
by which the most insignificant success is achieved."
~ Anne Sullivan ~

"Big doors swing on little hinges."
~ W. Clement Stone ~

"Get action. Seize the moment. Man was never intended
to become an oyster."
~ Theodore Roosevelt ~

"Do the difficult things while they are easy and so the great things while they are small. A journey of a thousand miles must begin with a single step."
~ Lao Tzu ~

"The miracle isn't that I finished.
The miracle is that I had the courage to start."
~ John Bingham ~

"This is a world of action, and not for moping and droning in."
~ Charles Dickens ~

Teamwork

"I love the feeling of being on a team, rehearsing together, sharing a dressing room—I love that so much."
~ Jennifer Garner ~

"I love being part of a company, and telling a story."
~ Judi Dench ~

"It's all so political. Keep the director happy. Keep the unit happy. Keep them working well. Because in the end, it's you up there on the screen."
~ Peter O'Toole ~

"You have to compromise all the way. The only thing that counts is the result."
~ Richard Widmark ~

"You cannot do everything at once, so find people you trust to help you. And don't be afraid to say no."
~ Jane Seymour ~

"If you only exercise your soloist muscles, the other muscles quickly atrophy."
~ Cate Blanchett ~

"I'd rather share the glory of a hit than star by myself in a flop."
~ Kate Jackson ~

"Something I learned in the Marine Corps that I've applied to acting is, one, taking direction, and then working with a group of people to accomplish a mission and knowing your role within that team."
~ Adam Driver ~

"You need a lot of different types of people to make the world better."
~ Joe Louis ~

"Snowflakes are one of nature's most fragile things, but just look what they can do when they stick together."
~ Vesta M. Kelly ~

"In my experience, committees can criticize, but they cannot create. 'Search the parks in all your cities. You'll find no statues of committees.'"
~ David Ogilvy ~

"Today, everything has to be made by committee, and has to have special effects, but there's always room for good films."
~ Robert Duvall ~

"When I'm wrongly cast, or in a poor script, I sink with the ship."
~ Gregory Peck ~

"Find a group of people who challenge and inspire you, spend a lot of time with them, and it will change your life."
~ Amy Poehler ~

"In an ideal way, in an ideal world, myself and the director are one. And as you rightly say, in an ideal world, you can't see the horizon between sky and sea. I felt that the times with Spielberg on *Schindler's List*, we were moving as one creature."
~ Ben Kingsley ~

"Every living being is an engine geared to the wheelwork of the universe. Though seemingly affected only by its immediate surrounding, the sphere of external influence extends to infinite distance."
~ Nikola Tesla ~

"The way a team plays as a whole determines its success. You may have the greatest bunch of individual stars in the world, but if they don't play together, the club won't be worth a dime."
~ Babe Ruth ~

"A group becomes a team when each member is sure enough of himself and his contribution to praise the skills of others."
~ Norman Shidle ~

"To collaborative team members, completing one another is more important than competing with one another."
~ John Maxwell ~

"In Australia, there aren't a lot of people committed to art, so these communities form that are dedicated to music, theater, cinema, but they're very small. So, they tend to move ahead on the power of collaboration, enthusiasm and creativity."
~ Joel Edgerton ~

Technique

"Love the art in yourself and not yourself in the art."
~ Constantin Stanislavski ~

"You'll begin to act when you can forget your technique—when it is so securely inside you that you need not call upon it consciously."
~ Stella Adler ~

"We learned our craft. Acting is a craft and you must learn it. I see a lot of talent today in the kids but they don't know how to work. They don't know the craft of acting and you can only get that on the stage in theater. You cannot learn how to act in movies or in television."
~ Jack Klugman ~

"Jack Nicholson is a textbook actor who's very intuitive. He is absolutely brilliant at going as far as you can go, always pushing to the edge, but still making it seem real."
~ Tim Burton ~

"A question you always ask in acting is, 'Where were you going if this scene didn't interrupt the movements of the character?'"
~ Jack Nicholson ~

"I used to tremble from nerves so badly that the only way I could hold my head steady was to lower my chin practically to my chest and look up at Bogie. That was the beginning of 'The Look.'"
~ Lauren Bacall ~

"Every part is approached in the same manner—gleaning all I can from what the author has written. When called for, I add reaction to any given circumstance such as I've witnessed and observed in others through life, applying the emotion in terms of the character as opposed to the way I might react personally."
~ Peter Cushing ~

"I'm an emotional actor. When I'm doing a scene, I really believe it. I live the part as long as I'm in the scene."
~ Victor Mature ~

"When you become the character you portray, it's the end of your career as an actor."
~ Basil Rathbone ~

"To me, acting is a matter of absolute concentration. You can laugh and giggle with your friends up to the minute the director says, 'Action!' Then you snap your mind into shape and into the character that you're playing and relate to the people that you're acting with and forget everybody else that you've been joking with."
~ Elizabeth Taylor ~

"Everyone can act. Everyone can improvise. Anyone who wishes to can play in the theater and learn to become stage-worthy."
~ Viola Spolin ~

"Acting is pretending that you're not pretending when you're actually pretending."
~ Ted Danson ~

"I was a guy who needed to go to class, because I had some raw talent that I thought was identifiable, when I finally made a decision to be an actor. And yet I wanted to learn how to really do the stuff. You know, 'How do I get to be a serious actor?'"
~ Jon Voight ~

"Acting is behaving truthfully under imaginary circumstances."
~ Sanford Meisner ~

"It's what I learn from the great actors that I work with. Stillness. That's all and that's the hardest thing."
~ Morgan Freeman ~

"If you can find a way your character moves, you know more about your character than you'd ever dream."
~ Rita Moreno ~

"Dialogue should simply be a sound among other sounds, just something that comes out of the mouths of people whose eyes tell the story in visual terms."
~ Alfred Hitchcock ~

"Acting is just a process of relaxation, actually. Knowing the text so well and trusting that the instinct and the subconscious mind, whatever you want to call it, is going to take over."
~ Anthony Hopkins ~

"I think acting is something that is within you. It's a very natural thing for me. It comes from myself, really."
~ Saoirse Ronan ~

"To you it looks emotionally straining, but I don't get emotionally drained, because I don't invest any of my real emotions. I don't take any of my characters' pain home with me, I don't even take it to craft services."

~ Jennifer Lawrence ~

"The real work of an actor goes on inside, and I don't think it changes from director to director—I always go for broke! But I don't get a lot of direction, unfortunately."

~ Ellen Burstyn ~

"She went right down into her own personal experience for everything, reached down and pulled something out of herself that was unique and extraordinary. She had no techniques. It was all the truth, it was only Marilyn. But it was Marilyn, plus. She found things, found things about womankind in herself."

~ John Huston ~

"All I try to do is to realize the man I'm playing fully, then put as much into my acting as I know how. To do it, I draw upon all that I've ever known, heard, seen or remember."

~ James Cagney ~

"I just try to be honest and true to the character and play the part."

~ Denzel Washington ~

"I always talk about my characters like they're real people."

~ Dakota Fanning ~

"Actors will say, 'My character wouldn't say that.'
Who said it was your character?"
~ *James Gandolfini* ~

"What are the aspects of yourself that line up with the character?
You magnify those, and the ones that don't match up you
kind of kick to the curb."
~ *Jeff Bridges* ~

"Acting is not about being someone different. It's finding
the similarity in what is apparently different,
then finding myself in there."
~ *Meryl Streep* ~

"Acting is a question of absorbing other people's personalities
and adding some of your own experiences."
~ *Paul Newman* ~

"I love trying to give some flesh to rather naked bones sometimes.
I've always felt it my duty and to try and bring on the character's
off-stage life, what happened that is not revealed."
~ *Christopher Plummer* ~

"It's not whether you really cry.
It's whether the audience thinks you are crying."
~ *Ingrid Bergman* ~

"Acting is experience with something sweet behind it."
~ *Humphrey Bogart* ~

"Part of my strength as an actor comes from what I've learned
all these years: when you play a villain, you try to get
the light touches; when you play a hero,
you try to get in some of the warts."
~ John Forsythe ~

"The horror thriller offers the serious actor unique opportunities
to test his ability to make the unbelievable believable."
~ Vincent Price ~

"And at NYU, I went to the Atlantic Theater Company,
and they have two main points. One of them is to always
be active in something instead of just feeling it.
And the other is figuring out your character."
~ Elizabeth Olsen ~

"I'd never ask an actor to do something I couldn't do—not that
I'm the best actor in the world—but if I can do it, then I know
that anyone I hire can do these things."
~ Rob Reiner ~

"I've acted with all types, I've directed all types.
What you want to understand as a director is what actors
have to offer. They'll get at it however they get at it.
If you can understand that, you can get your work done."
~ Ron Howard ~

"Good acting is thinking in front of the camera.
I just do that and apply a sense of humor to it.
You have to trust the audience to get it."
~ Charles Grodin ~

"Modeling teaches you to be completely conscious of the camera. Acting is being totally unconscious of it."
~ *Phoebe Cates* ~

"You need to find the size of performance that's appropriate to the material, appropriate to the shot, or appropriate to the scene."
~ *Jason Alexander* ~

"I'm not a Method actor. I don't believe acting should be psychodrama. I look within myself and see what I can find to play the role with."
~ *John Malkovich* ~

"I wouldn't say I'm a Method actor. I do research when I feel I don't have enough experience for the part I'm playing."
~ *Tim Robbins* ~

"I guess I'm probably a Method actor; I don't know … I just think of it as staying in the zone."
~ *Michael Keaton* ~

"The kids keep telling me I should try this new 'Method Acting' but I'm too old, I'm too tired and I'm too talented to care."
~ *Spencer Tracy* ~

"I'm afraid I probably outrage the Method people."
~ *Laurence Olivier* ~

"I don't know what I'm doing. I don't know what actors do."
~ *Geraldine Page* ~

"Method actors give you a photograph.
Real actors give you an oil painting."
~ Charles Laughton ~

"I can't articulate about the Method because I never studied it. I don't mean to suggest that I have any feelings one way or the other about it. I don't know what the Method is and I don't care what the Method is. Everybody's got a method. Everybody can't articulate about their method, and I can't, if I have a method—and Jane sometimes says that I use the Method, that is, the capital letter Method, without being aware of it. Maybe I do, it doesn't matter."
~ Henry Fonda ~

"If I were to play somebody who ran a fish and chip shop, I would not work in a fish and chip shop for three months. Staring at chips is not going to help me in my performance."
~ Ben Kingsley ~

"Theater acting is an operation with a scalpel; movie acting is an operation with a laser."
~ Michael Caine ~

"Pictures are much harder to do than the theater … you're at the mercy of the camera angles and the piecemeal technique."
~ Sydney Greenstreet ~

"I try to get inside a character and project him—one of my own private rules of thumb is that I have not got the character until I have mastered exactly how he walks."
~ Alec Guinness ~

Television

"I knew that nobody could be on television week after week as themselves and exist for any length of time, because no one has that rich a personality ... so I knew that I had to create some characters."
~ *Jackie Gleason* ~

"I hate television. I hate it as much as peanuts. But I can't stop eating peanuts."
~ *Orson Welles* ~

"Is there a grandmother that isn't spunky on television? Is there such a creature?"
~ *Rita Moreno* ~

"I've seen the invention of television and performed on television even before my family owned one."
~ *Carl Reiner* ~

"If I am writing a movie and I am stuck, I can call the studio and tell them it's delayed. You can't do that with television —you have air dates to meet."
~ *Aaron Sorkin* ~

"It has become a crusade of mine to demonstrate that TV need not be violent to be exciting."
~ *Gene Roddenberry* ~

"We want to prove that television, even in its half-hour form, can be both commercial and worthwhile. We want to tell stories that are different. At the same time, perhaps only as a side effect, a point can be made that the fresh and the untried can carry more infinite appeal than a palpable imitation of the already proved."
~ *Rod Serling* ~

"If it weren't for Philo T. Farnsworth, inventor of television, we'd still be eating frozen radio dinners."
~ *Johnny Carson* ~

"Television has done much for psychiatry by spreading information about it, as well as contributing to the need for it."
~ *Alfred Hitchcock* ~

"This instrument can teach, it can illuminate; yes, and even it can inspire. But it can do so only to the extent that humans are determined to use it to those ends. Otherwise, it's nothing but wires and lights in a box."
~ *Edward R. Murrow* ~

"Television offers a range and scope, and a degree of creativity and daring, that the bottom-line, global-audience-obsessed, brand-driven movie industry just can't compete with."
~ *Graydon Carter* ~

"You can't predict a show, that is the damndest thing, you can't predict if a show is going to work or not until it's on the air."
~ *Aaron Spelling* ~

"On the last day of our five-day work week, we did two performances and we had an audience. It was similar to theatre; we went from beginning to end, and it was very pleasing."
~ Jean Stapleton ~

"When I was doing *All in the Family*, half the time, I was looking at where the cameras were, where were the other actors in the scene, what the audience was doing."
~ Rob Reiner ~

"I want people to laugh and cry, not just sit and stare at the television. Maybe I'm old-fashioned, but I think viewers are hungry for shows in which people say something meaningful."
~ Michael Landon ~

"I would make the movie industry more like the television industry. TV is more material driven. In TV, you can break new stars. TV can take more chances."
~ Stephen Chbosky ~

"In television, you don't have a lot of time to spend with the role or the script. Typically you get a script a week prior to shooting. Sometimes it's even less time, not enough time to dream about the role."
~ Chadwick Boseman ~

"I've watched those shows my whole life—being on one is like a dream. It's hard to balance that dream with the fact that this is the Edie I've known my whole life."
~ Edie Falco ~

"Back then, it was more or less we couldn't change a line in our script. We weren't allowed to change lines. Today, actors change everything and won't do parts. It's very different today. Back then, the producers were in charge. Today, actors are more in charge."
~ **Donna Douglas** ~

"I don't think any industry was ever as closely scrutinized and written about and constantly in the public eye as television."
~ **Roone Arledge** ~

"I'm sometimes scared of everything that has happened to us. We didn't think Desilu Productions would grow so big. We merely wanted to be together and have two children."
~ **Lucille Ball** ~

"The second series is always my favorite as a writer-director; you can hit the ground running … so that's fun."
~ **Ricky Gervais** ~

"A lot of making TV is lightning in a bottle."
~ **Stephen J. Cannell** ~

"Every show has to be someone's favorite show."
~ **Brandon Tartikoff** ~

"In the history of pilot reports, *Seinfeld* has got to be one of the worst of all time."
~ **Warren Littlefield** ~

Theater

"The director, the stage designer, etc., are all accessories, but the actor is the theater."
~ Michael Chekhov ~

"The theater is so endlessly fascinating because it's so accidental. It's so much like life."
~ Arthur Miller ~

"I believe that in a great city, or even in a small city or a village, a great theatre is the outward and visible sign of an inward and probable culture."
~ Laurence Olivier ~

"Theatre is a mirror, a sharp reflection of society."
~ Yasmina Reza ~

"The word theatre comes from the Greeks. It means the seeing place. It is the place people come to see the truth about life and the social situation."
~ Stella Adler ~

"I regard the theatre as the greatest of all art forms, the most immediate way in which a human being can share with another the sense of what it is to be a human being."
~ Oscar Wilde ~

"Repertory theater is all about being part of the whole, one of the many colors in this vast palette."
~ Tom Hanks ~

"I love flexing theater muscles. Television has merits, as well, but there's no substitute for live theater."
~ Eddie Cahill ~

"I love the theater. I love the rehearsals. That's where you build a performance. That's your foundation. If you're gonna build a house, you start with the foundation. That makes the house strong. That's the way I build a character, from the foundation out."
~ Jack Klugman ~

"The performances you have in your head are always much better than the performances on stage."
~ Maggie Smith ~

"All I ever wanted to do was be on stage, if possible acting in Shakespeare. And to be as good as I could be."
~ Patrick Stewart ~

"I always, always meant to be on stage. I only ended up even auditioning for television and movies because I was understudying a Turgenev play on Broadway and was so broke that, when I got a mini-series, I had to take it and was so ashamed because I was such a snob."
~ Jennifer Garner ~

"When I emerged from drama school, I had no expectation that I would ever work in film."
~ *Cate Blanchett* ~

"I actually run a non-profit where one of the main objectives is to branch out and get a new audience for the theater. Just because the writing is so good and nothing is more effective than seeing something live and happening right in front of your face, so I definitely want to continue to pursue that."
~ *Adam Driver* ~

"It always bothered me when people came off stage and were told how great they were. They weren't, really, in my opinion. It was then I started thinking that, contrary to conventional wisdom, film was the artful medium for the actor, not the stage."
~ *Jack Nicholson* ~

"There are all sorts of reasons why I don't do much work in the theater, the main one being that after two performances I feel I've given all I can. I hate repetition, I really do. It's like asking a painter to paint the same picture every day of his life."
~ *Peter Cushing* ~

"And although I've been very fortunate in the film work that's come my way, I need to get back to the stage. If I'm away for a maximum of two years, I feel something's wrong."
~ *Ralph Fiennes* ~

"The theater was my mother and my father."
~ *Ingrid Bergman* ~

"I believe in the theater; I believe in it as the first glamorizer of thought. It restores dramatic dynamics and their relations to life size."
~ Laurence Olivier ~

"The whole thrust of theatre is different, just because the writing is so much more respected in a play. Whereas in movies—and having been the writer, I can say from experience—the writer is lower down on the food chain."
~ Matt Damon ~

"Broadway was without doubt the hardest I ever worked in my life and the highest highs I've ever had as an actor. The unadulterated fear was on a level that was hard to explain."
~ Brad Garrett ~

"I live halfway between reality and theater at all times. And I was born this way."
~ Lady Gaga ~

"Do some work in the theater if you can. It is the best training you can get."
~ Juliet Mills ~

"Anyone can do theater, even actors. And, theater can be done anywhere, even in a theater."
~ Augusto Boal ~

"Theater actors like to change character roles. They don't like to always do the same thing."
~ Marcello Mastroianni ~

"There's no getting away from the fact that theatre contains an element of hostility. Every actor knows that. Standing on the stage is an aggressive act. It says: Look at *me*. Listen to *me*. It says: I'm interesting, I'm talented, I'm remarkable."
~ Simon Callow ~

"In the theater, characters have to cut the umbilical cord from the writer and talk in their own voices."
~ Irwin Shaw ~

"To be true to a play, you can't add something that takes away from the author's intent."
~ Jason Robards ~

"A stage play ought to be the point of intersection between the visible and invisible worlds."
~ Arthur Adamov ~

"We live in what is, but we find a thousand ways not to face it. Great theatre strengthens our faculty to face it."
~ Thornton Wilder ~

"There's theater in life, obviously, and there's life in theater."
~ Charlie Kaufman ~

"Everything in life is theater."
~ Margo Jones ~

"When you end a successful sitcom, the most sensible thing to do is go back to the theater."
~ John Lithgow ~

Mike Kimmel

Thinking Bigger

"Some people think we're adrift without any guidelines.
I don't. I think we've had instruction on how to live."
~ Jon Voight ~

"If you want to change the world, you must be
your very best in your darkest moments."
~ Admiral William McRaven ~

"Reach high, for stars lie hidden in your soul.
Dream deep, for every dream precedes the goal."
~ Pamela Vault Starr ~

"We have our own truths to face all the time, unattractive and unappealing, so that it takes every ounce of imagination to create some sort of dream to hold on to, however foolish, however unlikely, however hidden. People live for their dreams, not for the oppressiveness of truths."
~ Michael Shurtleff ~

"There is no passion to be found playing small, in settling for a life that is less than the one you are capable of living."
~ Nelson Mandela ~

"I can do anything I set my mind to if I'm willing to pay the price for greatness."
~ Tom Bilyeu ~

"You lose yourself in something beyond yourself
and it's a lovely rest."
~ Dodie Smith ~

"Don't bunt. Aim out of the ballpark.
Aim for the company of immortals."
~ David Ogilvy ~

"He who makes a beast out of himself gets rid
of the pain of being a man."
~ Theodore Seuss Geisel ~

"Now consider this possibility—if you can figure it all out
on your own, then your dream may not be big enough!"
~ Jack Canfield ~

"Our Creator would never have made such lovely days
and have given us the deep hearts to enjoy them
unless we were meant to be immortal."
~ Nathaniel Hawthorne ~

"Acting should be bigger than life. Scripts should be
bigger than life. It should all be bigger than life."
~ Bette Davis ~

"Your gift will make room for you."
~ Steve Harvey ~

"Too much was never enough."
~ Waylon Jennings ~

Treating People Right

"I don't trust anyone who's nice to me but rude to the waiter.
Because they would treat me the same way
if I were in that position."
~ *Muhammad Ali* ~

"You can't stop being a citizen just because you have
a Screen Actors' Guild card."
~ *Paul Newman* ~

"You find with the really great actors, the ones you really
admire and look up to, very often they're very giving,
generous, warm people."
~ *Kit Harington* ~

"I respect the social graces enormously. How to pass the food.
Don't yell from one room to another. Don't go through a closed
door without a knock. Open the doors for the ladies. All these
millions of simple household behaviors make for a better life.
We can't live in constant rebellion against our parents—it's just
silly. I'm very well mannered. It's not an abstract thing.
It's a shared language of expectations."
~ *Jack Nicholson* ~

"To make a difference in someone's life, you don't have to be
brilliant, rich, beautiful, or perfect. You just have to care."
~ *Mandy Hale* ~

"Beginning today, treat everyone you meet as if they were going to be dead by midnight. Extend to them all the care, kindness and understanding you can muster, and do it with no thought of any reward. Your life will never be the same again."
~ Og Mandino ~

"You must ask yourself if you're standing up for what you know is right, if you're spending time with people close to you, if you're treating others with kindness and compassion. These questions are your moral compass, they're your North Star."
~ Forest Whitaker ~

"I think Barbra Streisand is a genius, the creativity she has! And I am very impressed with her as a person. Some years ago I was on the Academy Awards broadcast, she came up to me. I was standing in the wings and Barbra walked across the stage to greet me. Very polite, very nice. You don't find many young women who extend that kind of gracious courtesy to an older woman. Audrey Hepburn does. And Barbra. I've not forgotten how charming she was."
~ Myrna Loy ~

"People, even more than things, have to be restored, renewed, revived, reclaimed, and redeemed; never throw out anyone."
~ Audrey Hepburn ~

"Fans make you. I certainly hope that people like me in the work and I appreciate every letter that I get. I'm glad they like me or else I wouldn't be in the business."
~ Tanya Roberts ~

"I would like to be remembered as someone who accomplished useful deeds, and who was a kind and loving person. I would like to leave the memory of a human being with a correct attitude and who did her best to help others."
~ Grace Kelly ~

"When you handle yourself, use your head; when you handle others, use your heart."
~ Donna Reed ~

"Kindness and politeness are not overrated at all. They're underused."
~ Tommy Lee Jones ~

"I'm a fan of the fans. I love them. They're fabulous. I love being around them. I love their madness and their caring. I love watching them take off for a weekend, don the costumes, and become characters from the 23rd century and beyond. I thank the fans for giving us—me—so much support and love. I want them to know I love them. They will always be my friends. I'll see the fans, always. They can rest assured of that."
~ Nichelle Nichols ~

"Beautiful people have many advantages, but so do friendly people … I think beauty is an expression of love."
~ Lupita Nyong'o ~

"I just make it my business to get along with people so I can have fun. It's that simple."
~ Betty White ~

"How far you go in life depends on your being tender with the young, compassionate with the aged, sympathetic with the striving and tolerant of the weak and strong. Because someday in your life you will have been all of these."
~ George Washington Carver ~

"People will like you for the wrong reasons your entire life, even if you don't have parents who are celebrities. They will like you because you have a car or you have money or your breasts are big."
~ Susan Sarandon ~

"You don't like people because they're beautiful or they've got money or don't have money but because they're straight and honest and you feel at ease with them."
~ Lee Marvin ~

"The way you behave with everybody is more important than the work you do. Generosity, kindness and patience will get you so far: that's the biggest lesson I've learned."
~ Jake Gyllenhaal ~

"I'm not sure if I've learned anything from show business. Life in general has taught me if you're kind to people, everything gets easier. Being a decent person really smoothes the way for you and everyone else."
~ Alan Arkin ~

"Ninety per cent of acting is just not being obnoxious."
~ Marco Bottiglieri ~

Typecasting

"If I was as tough as I'm made out to be in movies,
I wouldn't have to worry."
~ Burt Reynolds ~

"I don't know why I always get to play these guys who have
few redeeming features. But don't knock it.
Villains are much more fun."
~ Joaquin Phoenix ~

"I did *Malice*, *Sommersby*, and *Sleepless in Seattle*, and they're
as disparate characters as I've ever played. But somehow,
there was that thing—they were all second male leads,
so they all didn't get the girl in some weird way."
~ Bill Pullman ~

"I seem always to have reminded people of someone
in their family. Perhaps I am the triumph of Plain Jane."
~ Helen Hayes ~

"My only problem is finding a way to play my fortieth
fallen female in a different way from my thirty-ninth."
~ Barbara Stanwyck ~

"When I look around the world, I don't see too many damsels
in distress. If they're a damsel in distress, they're manipulating
some guy to help them."
~ Sigourney Weaver ~

"It used to be that people thought I was Norm from *Cheers*. Ten years ago, everyone would say that to me. Then, in the last year, I was at a newsstand in Studio City, and I saw George Wendt. He said he had just gone on an audition, and they said they were looking for a Jeff Garlin type."
~ *Jeff Garlin* ~

"Scorsese and DeNiro taught me to bring out the natural side of myself. And they taught me to think of myself as the average guy. Sometimes the average guy belongs in a role more than your matinee idol-type of person. We have to have people we can relate to."
~ *Joe Pesci* ~

"They could never decide to their satisfaction what type I was. One would say, 'He's a heart-broken Byronic.' Another would say, 'No, he ain't; he's an all-American boy.' People began talking about Mitchum-type roles, but I still don't know what they mean."
~ *Robert Mitchum* ~

"With a name like Quinn, I wasn't totally accepted by the Mexican community in those days, and as a Mexican I wasn't accepted as an American. So as a kid I just decided, well, ' A plague on both your houses. I'll just become a world citizen.' So that's what I did. Acting is my nationality."
~ *Anthony Quinn* ~

"Typecasting is a good thing. It's good to be known for what you do."
~ *Steve Guttenberg* ~

"I have played Polynesian. I have played an Arabian girl.
I played an East Indian girl. And what was so confusing …
is that I assumed I had to have an accent. Nobody said
anything, so I made up what I call the universal ethnic accent,
and they all sounded alike. It didn't matter who I was playing."
~ *Rita Moreno* ~

"In the early days I played a lot of comedy in the theater
and on television. But once an actor becomes well known in
any kind of part, he tends to get stereotyped. After I played
Frankenstein, I was only thought of in that light. Of course,
some actors are better at drama and some are better at comedy.
But they can certainly have a stab at both.
An actor should be able to do it all."
~ *Peter Cushing* ~

"I'm not crazy. I play a lot of crazy characters, but I'm an actor."
~ *Randy Quaid* ~

"I don't want to be known as this goody-two-shoes who can
only do comedies where puppies are licking
peanut butter off my face."
~ *Kevin James* ~

"If you need a ceiling painted, a chariot race run, a city
besieged, or the Red Sea parted, you think of me."
~ *Charlton Heston* ~

"Just call me a nice, clean-cut Mongolian boy."
~ *Yul Brynner* ~

Visualization

"The actor should be able to create the universe in the palm of his hand."
~ Laurence Olivier ~

"Life is to be lived within the limits of your knowledge and within the concept of what you would like to see yourself to be."
~ Burt Lancaster ~

"The key questions are: Which mental state would be most useful in this situation? And which version of reality would help you get there?"
~ Olivia Fox Cabane ~

"You act like the kind of person you imagine yourself to be. It's as simple as that."
~ Jack Foster ~

"Whatever the mind is set upon, or whatever it keeps most in view, that it is bringing to it, and the continual thought or imagining must at last take form and shape in the world of seen and tangible things."
~ Prentice Mulford ~

"Genius is the ability to put into effect what is in your mind. There's no other definition of it."
~ F. Scott Fitzgerald ~

"The thing you set your mind on is the thing
you ultimately become."
~ *Nathaniel Hawthorne* ~

"You become what you think about all day long."
~ *Ralph Waldo Emerson* ~

"We become what we think about, but the thinking is up to us."
~ *Earl Nightingale* ~

"Everything you can imagine is real."
~ *Pablo Picasso* ~

"People who can't see it for themselves can't see it for you."
~ *Les Brown* ~

"Films are developed in the dark; likewise, mental pictures
are developed in the darkroom of the subconscious mind."
~ *Dr. Joseph Murphy* ~

"Everything's in the mind. That's where it all starts.
Knowing what you want is the first step toward getting it."
~ *Mae West* ~

"Life is a mirror and will reflect back to the thinker
what he thinks into it."
~ *Ernest Holmes* ~

"You can't depend on your eyes
when your imagination is out of focus."
~ *Mark Twain* ~

A Request

If you've enjoyed *The Actor's Book of Quotes*—and feel that it would benefit our fellow actors and teachers—then please consider leaving a short book review on the merchant site where you purchased it (or your favorite book-review website and/or online retailer).

Book reviews are extremely important for both authors and readers. They are very much appreciated by both. Reviews help spread the word to readers looking for new material in a specific genre, and also help authors reach a larger readership. Even one brief line or two makes a very big difference.

Additionally, please consider recommending this book to your local public library or school library. Schools and libraries can often purchase books at a significant discount. In this way, the book can be made available to readers who may not be able to purchase their own copies.

Mike Kimmel

Performing Arts Books in this Series

Youngsters

Acting Scenes for Kids and Tweens
Monologues for Kids and Tweens
Monologues for Kids and Tweens II

Teenagers

Scenes for Teens
Monologues for Teens
Monologues for Teens II
One-Minute Monologues for Teens

College and Adult

Monologues for Adults
Monologues for Young Adults
Six Critical Essays on Film
The Actor's Book of Quotes

About Mike Kimmel

Mike Kimmel is a former pro wrestler and circus magician. Nowadays, he is a film, television, stage, and commercial actor and acting coach. He is a twenty-plus year member of SAG-AFTRA with extensive experience in both the New York and Los Angeles markets.

He has worked with directors Francis Ford Coppola, Robert Townsend, Craig Shapiro, and Christopher Cain among many others. Television credits include *Game of Silence, Zoo, Treme, In Plain Sight, Cold Case, Breakout Kings, Memphis Beat, Buffy The Vampire Slayer, One Life to Live, Up All Night with Gilbert Gottfried,* and *The Oprah Winfrey Show.* He was a regular sketch comedy player on *The Tonight Show,* performing live on stage and in pre-taped segments with Jay Leno for eleven years.

Mike is a full voting member of the National Academy of Television Arts and Sciences, the organization that produces The Emmy Awards. He has taught at seven colleges and universities and four public school districts throughout the United States. He now divides his time between Los Angeles, California and Albuquerque, New Mexico.

www.ingramcontent.com/pod-product-compliance
Lightning Source LLC
Chambersburg PA
CBHW071958110526
44592CB00012B/1134